A CURIOUS
FUTURE

2ND EDITION

A CURIOUS FUTURE

A Handbook of Unusual
Divination and Unique Oracular Techniques

By
KIKI DOMBROWSKI

Witch Way Publishing

Second Edition, 2021

Tonya A. Brown
3436 Magazine St
#460
New Orleans, LA 70115
www.witchwaypublishing.com

Editor: Tonya A. Brown
Assistant Editor: Paul Flagg
Cover Designer: Johnny Dombrowski
Illustrator: Haley Newman
Internal Design: Emily Barta

Printed in the United States of America

ISBN 978-0578855028

For Jessica Robbins:
She was an amazing woman who always supported my writing
and correctly predicted future events at the time of my birth.

CONTENTS

A CURIOUS
FUTURE

*O*RACLE. *PROPHET. SEER. MYSTIC.* THESE ARE JUST A handful of the titles given to those able to see beyond what is in front of them. By using psychic abilities, intuition, and divinatory tools, humans are able to see into the future or the past, to recognize when the world is showing them omens, and interact with a mysterious universe, allowing them to lead a profoundly spiritual life and have a deep connection with themselves, others, and divinity. Divination works as an access card to a deeply spiritual life of divine work and soulful awareness.

Maybe you have picked up this book because you want to begin learning how to use divination in your life. Maybe you have picked up this book because you want to expand your knowledge base and learn about different methods of divination, psychic enhancement, fortune telling, and exploring omens to foretell events outside of your own perspective. My hope is that this book will help you understand that the realm of divination is an ancient and extensive one with limitless possibilities.

WHAT IS DIVINATION?

The word divination comes from the Latin word *divinare*, which means "to foresee" and "to be inspired by God." Divination is the practice of observing symbols to gain information about the unknown or the future. Divination is done with a variety of tools, and as you will see, just about every*thing* has been used across civilizations and cultures to try to gain insight and clarity into situations that cannot be perceived from the present perspective. It is a gateway to deepening your understanding of yourself and both the visible and invisible world around you.

It is hard to categorize the vast ways divination is practiced. In some cases, special objects are created with particular symbols on them and a divination reading is created from interpreting how those tools are cast. In other cases, the patterns that occur in natural objects will be examined or observed and used to create a divination reading. And one step beyond this, sometimes people receive messages that come through in omens, dreams, or premonitions. Divination has a rich and varied history, and you may discover a form that you connect with then choose to devote your time to through exploration, research, and practice. This book will give you the information you need to work with many different forms of divination and determine which resonate most with you.

HISTORY OF DIVINATION

Divination is not a new fad that popped up with the rise of modern witchcraft. As a matter of fact, as long as there was human civilization, there was some form of divination being practiced. Divination is part of the human experience: people from cultures worldwide found ways to seek out divine messages to help them make thoughtful decisions and understand their place in the universe better. The ancient Babylonians created astrology. In Egypt, various forms of divination were practiced, such as scrying and capnomancy, or divination with smoke. In Greece, the Oracle of Delphi gave omens. Ancient Romans preferred haruspicy, which is the divination of observing animal entrails. Tacitus observed Germanic and Celtic tribes using wooden sticks for divination. In Tibet, turtle shells were thrown onto fires then removed in order to read cracks in the shells that were said to reveal divinatory messages. In African tribes, shells and nuts were thrown, and the shape these materials created would be interpreted.

TYPES OF DIVINATION

† CASTING OF LOTS: To cast lots means to throw specially selected objects and develop interpretations and predictions based on how and where they land. Casting of lots is a popular and common means of divining and indicates that an object is used to create an omen. You may have heard someone say "throw the bones" or "cast the stones" to poetically describe the process of taking out and using their divination tools for a reading. Think of casting of lots as anything that requires the drawing, casting, or throwing of an object then using that object to produce a reading. Therefore, it's an extensive term, capturing divination types, including (but not limited to) using bones, crystals, trinkets, shells, dice, runes, and cards.

† SIGNS AND OMENS: Signs and omens are a means of divination when you create predictions based on your surroundings. In other words, you may see symbols, images, or events that you then interpret as a divine message. Examples of signs and omens may include the motion of incense smoke, seeing a number repeatedly, or overhearing a lyric in a song that you construe as a message.

† VISIONS AND PREMONITIONS: Visions and premonitions represent divination through psychic visions and intuitive gut feelings. This may include visions in channeling, mediumship, and psychometry. Many people feel that they receive premonitions and divine messages in their dreams. You may also see visions while scrying into a reflective surface.

YOU CAN USE DIVINATION

Simply put, anyone can use divination and this book is for everyone. While many Pagans, Wiccans, and witches enjoy using divination, it is not limited to those who practice these spiritual modalities and belief systems.

Likewise, divination is not an evil practice by any means, and if done from a mindful place of good intention, it can amplify your own intuitive and spiritual practices while helping to support and encourage others. There is a form of divination that you are going to love, and there are forms of divination you will have no interest in. No system of divination is superior to another, so you should feel comfortable working with the systems that you feel most drawn to. You will find there are forms of divination you use regularly, while there are other forms you like to use only at certain times of the year.

This is going to be a powerful and personal journey. Divination will help you access mystical and magical powers within yourself, helping you tap into those same forces that deepen your connection to yourself, others, and the world around you. Working with divination doesn't simply mean being able to select lottery numbers, seeing precisely measured events of the faraway future, or locating a missing object; rather, it is about magical empowerment. It is about contemplating deeper questions, seeking out the esoteric to activate your higher self, and finding spiritual solutions to help you walk the most beneficial and creative paths. You can use divination to deepen your connection to spirituality, discover inspiration when you are feeling stagnant, and support you in understanding yourself and the world (and otherworld) around you.

A LITTLE ABOUT MYSELF

I have known about my magical side since I was a little girl. As a child I would have vivid dreams, imaginary friends, and even memories of past lives. This certainly didn't make things easy growing up—I was frequently the target of bullying for the way I looked, my last name, and my peculiar demeanor. This drove me even deeper into a magical and solitary world where I felt the most comfort in nature and in my dreams.

Around the time I was thirteen years old, I received my first tarot deck and have been reading regularly since then, exploring how certain cards would translate into real-life events. I started studying witchcraft, then incorporated celebrating the sabbats and lunar cycles into my life. In my early twenties I found a small shop in Connecticut where I began to read for the public and take courses on Wicca, witchcraft, and divination. I studied mediumship and offered sessions to small groups of people, delighted to see that there was a positive response. One of my favorite memories was of connecting with a young spirit guide of mine. When she appeared, the candles at the table at which we were hosting the session began to flicker high. Far off, as if from a room away, we could all hear an audible sound of a girl giggling. I found I loved mediumship and channeling and decided to study and practice divination as a way to expand my psychic abilities and deepen my spirituality. I always found ways to weave divination and spirituality into my life. Runes were a form of divination I was very drawn to, and I eventually wrote my undergraduate honors thesis on where spiritual practitioners and academics' interpretations of the runes intersected.

It was actually my love for runes and runic interpretations that led me to my next big writing opportunity with *Witch Way Magazine*, where I began to frequently contribute to the monthly issues with articles on varying forms of divination. Since then, I have gathered and collected many wonderful divination kits—from quirky tarot decks to profoundly personal trinket kits and everything in between. I have found so much pleasure in helping clients through divination readings and in teaching others that they can access so much insightful information through divination. My hope is that this book will support you in your own exploration.

NEW CONTENTS IN THIS EDITION

This book was originally published a couple of years ago. Since then, I have continued to work with the forms of divination closely in this book and have been excited to share my deeper discoveries and continued research. You will find that each section has expanded information. Divination, however, isn't just a practice in research: it is a practice in personal experience. With that in mind, I have included my personal notes and experiences with divination, sharing with you the contents of various divination kits I have built and worked with since writing the first edition of *A Curious Future*. I have chosen to do this because it feels so powerful to work with a divination kit that I created from scratch. I'm also excited to share with you interviews from divination experts, people I know and respect who work professionally as psychics and have extensive knowledge of specialty divination.

NOTES: THE LITTLE THINGS TO KEEP IN MIND MOVING FORWARD

You are going to find that this book is something you can flip through and visit as a reference for a variety of divination practices. Please understand moving forward that this book strives to examine and work with unusual forms of divination and create methods for you to use them. This book is inspired by unique forms of divination and finding ways to use them in our modern world. You may find that insight from this book can be used in conjunction with more familiar forms of divination. There are plenty of tarot readers who use pendulums over cards, for example. Or you may want to incorporate tea leaf reading into an astrology session. The opportunities are limitless, and you'll find, through practice and exploration, which methods are most complimentary for what you wish to accomplish.

My hope is that you can use this book as a springboard to deepen your connection to fascinating and curious forms of divination. The divination highlighted in this book may be new to you—I know in writing this book I discovered plenty of new information as well. Find what you enjoy, explore it, try it out, and repeat. You will find that there is an extensive bibliography at the end of the book with references I sourced but also recommend for the time you are ready to take even deeper dives into divination.

CHAPTER ONE

GETTING STARTED:

Navigating Psychic Abilities, Development, and Practice

T O BEGIN, I WANT TO INVITE YOU TO explore your psychic abilities and tune into your intuition as a way to really support your divination practice. In this section, you will discover different ways to enhance psychic abilities through a variety of exercises and meditations.

Psychic abilities may feel very natural to some, while for others they may feel like something foreign, as if only a few individuals possess the ability to tap into psychic powers; however, everyone can tap into their own sixth sense. Sometimes the most difficult thing to do is to be quiet enough to hear or sense psychic messages then feel confident enough to believe them to be useful or profound. This all comes with practice, and over time, you may feel more comfortable and confident listening to these psychic voices. If this is your first time delving into the world of psychic abilities, start slow, research often, take notes, and try out some of the exercises listed in this chapter.

EMPATHY, INTUITION,
OR PSYCHIC ABILITIES?

You may hear three terms often when working with divination and premonitions: EMPATHY, INTUITION, and PSYCHIC ABILITIES.

† EMPATHY is when you personally feel what someone else is going through, an emotional response to another person's emotional response. Have you ever felt like you were in someone else's shoes to the point where you can feel that perspective as if it was your own? That's empathy. An empath is sensitive to the energy of places and the feelings or attitudes people around them experience. It is a blessing to have empathy, being able to connect with and relate to someone, but at times it can be exhausting and draining—ask any empath who works in a toxic environment!

† INTUITION also feels like a soulful, emotional experience but is perhaps one step further than empathy since there is a predictive element to it. Intuition can be described as an instinctive gut feeling that pulls you toward or pushes you away from doing something.

† PSYCHIC ABILITIES are a little more multifaceted, sometimes revealing clear information and details about events or circumstances or offering cryptic hints that lead you down a path of trying to understand and interpret the meaning of the message given. Both intuition and psychic abilities tap into something that goes beyond our "normal five senses."

WHICH "CLAIR" ARE YOU?

You may be familiar with the "CLAIRS"—clairvoyance, clairsentience, and clairaudience—but what do they mean? Which do you possess? And what can you do to develop them? The "clair-abilities" are a way to distinguish and categorize different psychic abilities and premonitions. Some people use them to describe what kind of psychic experiences they have or use in their own practices. You may have experienced all of the clair-abilities or feel that you resonate with one kind over another. Let's take a look at the different clairs and consider ways to tap into your already magical psychic abilities.

† CLAIRSENTIENCE literally means "clear feeling." It means being able to feel psychic premonitions and sensing something to be valuable information. When you are experiencing clairsentience, you may get goosebumps when you speak about something spiritually powerful, or you may feel uncomfortable in a haunted or unwelcoming environment. The other day, I felt a warm, soothing feeling while being around someone who was loving and kind. Perhaps, in a way, clairsentience is our body's way of intuitively reacting to our surroundings, allowing us to feel who or what resonates with us.

Clairsentience can be developed by working with a pendulum (page 96) or with psychometry (page 121) more broadly. You may also use dowsing rods to see whether you can follow a line of energy through a natural setting or park. On a smaller scale, see if you feel led to a certain area in your home or garden, meditating on why you were led to that specific area. Pay attention to how your body responds to being in a new place, as you may just "know" information about that environment during your first walk-through.

† CLAIRAUDIENCE is "clear hearing" and means being able to hear psychic premonitions, an inner voice, song, or sound. You may hear words and numbers that seem to come into your mind without explanation. These words give direction or premonition. Or you may feel you have communicated with other people, animals, or plants, even though you are not speaking. As a tarot reader, I have sometimes touched a card during a reading and "heard" in my mind a word or sometimes even a song.

Clairaudience can be developed by learning how to listen. Try going out into nature, resting comfortably, closing your eyes, and paying close attention to the sounds you hear. You may also want to work with psychometry, touching a crystal, flower, or tree and listen for a message.

If you have a friend or relative you feel very connected to, see if they would like to practice clairaudience with you by attempting to "listen" to each other's thoughts. Have your psychic buddy repeat a word or phrase in his or her mind and listen for it. My editor and friend, a brilliant witch, Tonya A. Brown also suggests an interesting exercise: tune a radio or television to a fuzzy station that is playing white noise. See if you can hear any clairaudient messages come through the static.

† CLAIRVOYANCE is "clear seeing" and means being able to see psychic premonitions that appear as visions or images in your mind. You may see people, places, events, or scenes in your mind while your eyes are closed. They may be vivid or symbolic in nature, but they usually always leave a lasting impression, such as when you feel as though you've visited a place through the images in your mind despite never having been there before.

You can develop clairvoyance through a number of psychic practices. You may want to try scrying (page 171), aura reading (page 44), or even ESP (extrasensory perception) cards. A fun (and sometimes silly) activity I've asked my students is to visualize my desk and describe what they see on it. You may want to try this with a close friend or in a workshop of your own. If you are a tarot or oracle card reader, draw a card and set it face down in front of you. Place your hand on the card and try to visualize the scene on the card.

OTHER CLAIRS

Some people use other clair-categories to further distinguish psychic abilities. They are abilities we may not hear about as frequently and may even consider a little unusual. You may, however, be surprised to have experienced some of them at one time or another.

† CLAIRALIENCE is "clear smelling," when you smell a familiar fragrance but cannot link it to an actual source. Some people say they have smelled the perfume of a relative who has passed and believe the scent is a sign of their

presence. In nature, you may be blasted by the smell of a beautiful bouquet of flowers, perhaps an indication that nature spirits or the Fae are close by.

† CLAIRGUSTANCE is "clear tasting," when you can taste something even though you have nothing in your mouth.

† CLAIRCOGNIZANCE is "clear knowing," when you feel you just know something to be true without validation, often accompanied by a gut feeling or an "intuitive hit."

MEDITATING WITH
YOUR CLAIR-ABILITY

MEDITATION is the practice of calming and centering the mind and body to feel more aware of the present moment. It can be a rewarding spiritual practice that can also help you access your clair-abilities while allowing you to cultivate a deeper sense of self through reflection. There are many different types of meditation worth exploring.

† MINDFUL MEDITATION can help you feel deeply aware of your present state by focusing on the breath and allowing passing thoughts to dissolve or pass by in an effort to return to the present moment. It allows you to slow down, focus on your body, and become more aware of internal sounds and visions.

† MOVEMENT MEDITATION invites you to engage in a peaceful activity, such as performing a repetitive task to let your mind go into a meditative or an introspective space. I have found that you can do this while walking, doing yoga, gardening, and even cleaning dishes.

† MANTRA MEDITATION is a meditation in which you repeat a mantra, phrase, or word in order to focus. This phrase can be something you wish to work on or invite into your life.

† VISUALIZATION MEDITATION focuses on visualizing a specific image or experience. Meditation of any kind can support you in awakening any psychic abilities. I personally enjoy listening to guided visualization mediations led by someone who suggests certain images and experiences to visualize with your mind's eye. Through a guided meditation, you are sent along a psychic journey where you can develop your clair-abilities on a more spiritual level. I have personally found that my sixth sense is awake and I am more sensitive psychically and magically when I meditate regularly. Consider beginning a psychic session with a small meditation to awaken your clair-abilities.

Close your eyes, and in your mind, envision each of your chakras, starting at the root and going up to the crown, spinning clockwise and growing brighter. Visualize white light energy protecting you.

In your mind, say the word "clairsentience," and when you do so, feel a warmth of knowing come over you.

Next, in your mind, say the word "clairaudience." When you do so, feel your ears perk up, opening to clear, accurate, and beneficial messages.

Finally, in your mind, say the word "clairvoyance." When you do so, visualize your third eye opening, seeing beyond where you sit and meditate, focusing in on images that are vivid, thoughtful, and beneficial.

When you are ready, begin your practice.

This is just a simple meditation, and perhaps over time you will experience different sensations and visions when you open yourself to the clair-abilities in this way.

PREPARING FOR PSYCHIC WORK

You'll hear me repeat this a few times, but it is with great emphasis that I suggest the idea of practicing moments of silence and meditation in your daily routine. Meditation allows the mind to shift into a quiet observational space, one in which you are aware of your feelings and mindful of your surroundings. Even if you only take a few minutes out of your day to gently meditate, you may find you feel calmer and more in tune with yourself. You can even try a small meditation right now:

Pay attention to your breath. Let your belly fill with air and slowly release your breath. Honor the thoughts that come through your mind and release them when you breath out.

Keeping a meditation practice in the technological world can be tricky, but there are also many resources online to help you meditate. I am obsessed with an app called Insight Timer, which features an extensive collection of meditations, including some to help open the third eye, which is a chakra or energy point located in the center of your forehead between your eyes. It is the center of mystical perception and intuitive insight. As you meditate, keep a journal nearby so you can make note of any gut feelings, internal voices, premonitions, synchronicities, and so on that you may encounter. See how they play into the routine of developing comfort with, and listening to, your inner voice.

Some people like to perform a small protective ritual before practicing divination and psychic abilities. This is done to keep what is psychically yours to yourself and what belongs to others to themselves. One method of protection that many people in the psychic and holistic worlds are familiar with is known as the "white light bubble." This is a way to create a boundary around yourself (and those you are working with) to prevent anything harmful from entering.

Sit in a comfortable position with both feet on the ground and close your eyes. Breathe in slowly—in through your nose, then out through your mouth.

With your mind's eye, visualize a bright white light surrounding you. Envision this light creating a shield around you.

Many psychics and sensitives also like to create a protective boundary with sea salt wherever they are doing their work. This is a common practice during rituals, magic work, clairvoyant work, and medium sessions. Some also like to cleanse their bodies with herbal wands before and after psychic work.

An opening meditation to begin your psychic work:

Rest in a meditative state and with every breath visualize your body feeling warm and grounded.

Visualize white light surrounding you. Next, visualize pulling a thick, velvet indigo cloak over your shoulders.

Say to yourself, "I welcome love and light into my circle of divination. May my intuition be strong and true."

PSYCHIC ENHANCING TOOLS

CRYSTALS contain energy that can assist with different vibrations. My recommendation is to work with the crystals you are most drawn to. One psychic exercise you may want to try with your crystal is to hold one with your eyes closed and see if you sense an energy or associated uses and properties. On the following pages are some of my favorite crystals to have nearby when I am doing divination and psychic work, as well as some of the traditionally identified energies of each crystal.

AMETHYST: Amethyst is said to have a soothing quality, bringing both peaceful and spiritual energies to a space. It is an excellent crystal to hold during meditation and is known to help awaken psychic abilities. You can hold a piece of amethyst while you are meditating.

ANGELITE: I will keep a piece of angelite by my bedside if I am hoping to have vivid dreams. Angelite is said to assist in feeling compassion and gentle love but also said to open communication between yourself and spiritual or angelic guides.

APATITE: Apatite is an excellent stone for psychics who need an extra boost in getting visions and messages to materialize. Keep with larimar and aquamarine to connect with the magic of Atlantis and Lemuria.

AQUA AURA QUARTZ: I've always connected aqua aura quartz to The Star card in tarot, as it has an etheric and glimmering quality to it that both awakens psychic abilities and relieves the carrier of tension.

AZURITE: Azurite can make you feel very aware of your intuition and support psychic abilities. According to Naisha Ahsian in *The Book of Stones*, "Azurite is a classic ally for the psychic, medium, channel, or other intuitive Light worker. It enhances one's psi powers and helps one maintain objectivity and accuracy," (94). I have always kept a piece of azurite with merlinite to work with ancient wisdom.

BLUE CHALCEDONY: Blue Chalcedony has a very calming effect and can especially assist those who are channeling or wish to share their psychic information in a gentle healing demeanor.

BLUE KYANITE: Blue Kyanite can assist in improving psychic dreams and visions, assist in astral projection, and awaken psychic abilities.

Crystal Quartz: Crystal quartz points are like antennae, as they can help to amplify and enhance energy. Keep a crystal quartz with your divination kit to help clear energy after work sessions.

Dumortierite: This lesser known, yet readily available, deep blue crystal can help you access precise and accurate psychic information. It helps to lift mental fog and connect with divine wisdom. Hold on to fluorite and dumortierite when you are learning new divination or practicing divination.

Labradorite: Labradorite is such a magical crystal and one that awakens a connection to all things otherworldly, spiritual, and mystical. I have a couple beautiful pieces of labradorite and, at an office job a couple of years ago, would carry one around with me. It would be passed along between colleagues, all of whom loved to feel its energy because it would give them etheric departure from the tense and unnatural corporate space we were in.

Lapis Lazuli: Lapis lazuli has a long history of being revered for its beauty and energies. It is considered a powerful crystal for psychics, assisting in connecting to divinity and opening the third eye. It can help the bearer access psychic abilities through meditation, dreams, and trance.

Merlinite: According to Robert Simmons in *The Book of Stones*, "Merlinite can part the veils between the visible and invisible worlds, opening the doors to deeper intuitive abilities" (307). I have an orb of merlinite, which I like to keep on display. It's a stunning piece I like to use in crystal grids with pieces of bluestone, the type of stone used to build Stonehenge.

Moonstone: Moonstone is a feminine crystal, aligned with the spiritual properties of the moon. The stone supports intuition, meditation, and psychic awareness.

SELENITE: Selenite is a powerful crystal for empaths and those who are sensitive. It is a soothing stone and supports the purification of energy. Keep a piece of selenite with your divination kit to clear any residual energy that has been collected on it.

SIBERIAN BLUE QUARTZ: While this stone is lesser known than some of the others in this list, it is one of my favorites and one of the few I have felt a very powerful pull toward. Like aqua aura quartz, this crystal is a lab-created stone. Siberian blue quartz can help activate psychic abilities and is a comforting stone for those who feel like they are Starseeds, people who are deeply aligned with the cosmos and feel a soulful connection to the heavens.

SODALITE: Sodalite has a soft, mellow energy that will assist with accessing psychic abilities, especially if you channel or receive clairvoyant messages. The energy of sodalite is gentle and comforting. I personally like to keep sodalite on me when I have busy reading days to help keep me calm and in a peaceful head-space. If you are feeling cloudy or ungrounded after doing many readings, hold a piece of sodalite in one hand and a piece of smoky quartz in the other while visualizing yourself anchoring to the ground.

SUGILITE: Keep a piece of sugilite and angelite by your bedside to have vivid dreams with profound messages. Cassandra Eason in her book *Healing Crystals* suggests using sugilite to "contact spirit guides and light beings, and for an awareness of other dimensions" (142).

SUPER SEVEN: Super Seven is said to enhance psychic abilities. It activates the third eye and can make the holder feel more aware of their clairvoyant and clairaudient powers. It is believed to support channelers in receiving deep and profound messages.

CRYSTAL GRID FOR
ACTIVATING DIVINATION TOOLS

This crystal grid can be used to activate divination tools by using stones associated with psychic energy. If you don't have all of the crystals to build this elaborate grid, that is okay. Instead, surround your kit with a combination of any of the above listed crystals and place it under the full moonlight.

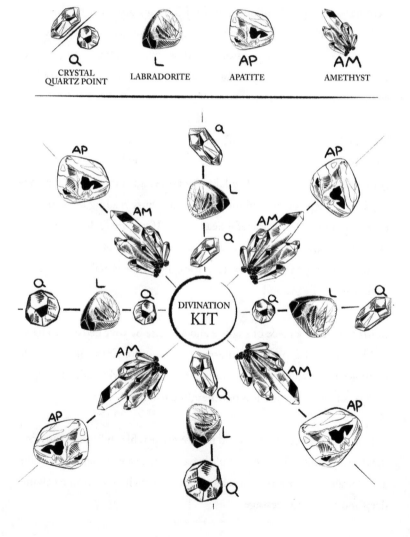

Q
CRYSTAL
QUARTZ POINT

L
LABRADORITE

AP
APATITE

AM
AMETHYST

ESSENTIAL OILS FOR DIVINATION

There are many ESSENTIAL OILS that are associated with psychic abilities and are said to awaken the sixth sense and assist in enhancing divination sessions. Some of my favorites include anise, bay, benzoin, bergamot, cinnamon, clary sage, geranium, lemongrass, jasmine, orange, and sandalwood.

In the original version of this book, I included an old oil blend recipe for divination from my book of shadows, which is a special book of collected magical work, spells, research, and rituals. Since then, I have started to use an updated recipe that I am sharing with you here because it has a lovely, enchanting fragrance that I love to wear when doing divination. I find that any time I smell it, my mind and spirit know it is time to shift into psychic and divination work. The following recipe is made to fit a four-dram bottle. Begin by slowly adding the essential oils and top off with a carrier oil—I prefer using fractionated coconut oil.

DIVINATION OIL BLEND

- 16 DROPS AMBER
- 14 DROPS CLARY SAGE
- 7 DROPS BERGAMOT
- 10 DROPS BAY
- 6 DROPS ANISE

- 6 DROPS GERANIUM
- 3 DROPS CINNAMON

OPTIONAL: Add a pinch of mugwort and yarrow, along with a small amethyst piece, to the bottle.

PSYCHIC INCENSE

INCENSE can be an extra tool to enhance psychic abilities and cleanse, purify, or protect the area where you are doing work. Incense with sandalwood, amber, cinnamon, and mugwort can help raise psychic energies. A simple incense blend for charging divination tools can be made with equal parts of frankincense, sandalwood, mugwort, benzoin, and a dash of cinnamon. If you prefer not to burn herbs and resins, consider getting an oil burner and simmering oils and herbs. Oils that can help with psychic energies include peppermint, jasmine, lemongrass, anise, honeysuckle, and rose. Some people claim that a tea with mugwort and cinnamon before bedtime can enhance psychic abilities and dreams as well.

PSYCHIC TEA

Here is another recipe I found in that same book of shadows that you may enjoy if you are a tea drinker. Brew the following herbs together to create a cup of tea to help enhance psychic abilities:

- 1 TSP. JASMINE GREEN TEA
- ¼ TSP. CALENDULA
- ¼ TSP. DANDELION
- ¼ TSP. MUGWORT

FIONA HORNE
ON PSYCHIC INTUITION

Fiona Horne, author of *Witch: A Magickal Journey* and *The Art of the Witch*, is one of my favorite authors in the witchcraft community. I have had the honor of spending time with her on a couple of different trips to New Orleans for HexFest. In 2017, she led a course on psychic intuition and brought up many great points that still resonate with me to this day. More specifically, she had us identify our reactions to intuitive hits.

You may hear negative thoughts when you are trying to work with your psychic abilities. There may be self-doubt, and you may wonder if you are making up the premonitions in your head. There may be other negative feelings as well, such as fear, guilt, shame, or pride. Fiona points out that even these negative feelings offer our body chemical rewards. In other words, when we worry, our body rewards us with feeling like we are doing something.

What Fiona suggests is to identify good feelings with intuitive hits. Identify the feelings and sensations you have when you are having a psychic or intuitive experience. Be thankful for the psychic and intuitive moments and celebrate the feeling that it gives you to sense something so unique and special. Seeking out gratitude during this work can be the best way to help with intuition, as gratitude stimulates dopamine production in the brain. So, not only will being grateful make you feel good, but it can be something you use in readings as a means to feel greater intuition and show gratitude for psychically connecting with others.

Fiona reminded us of the saying "When I gave up being a perfectionist suddenly everything became perfect." Being a perfectionist can shut down your ability to give psychic information. If you are expecting flawless, groundbreaking psychic omens each time you do divination, you may find yourself disappointed. Celebrate the process of learning divination and learn how to identify when you have made a clear and valid psychic prediction or interpretation.

SHOW ME A SIGN!

Tune into the world around you and see if there are any messages that reveal themselves to you. Ask the universe, source, or divinity to grant you psychic clarity and show you signs and omens. As simple as it sounds, sometimes just asking to be shown a sign can be an effective way of initiating psychic work. Perhaps you will see a repetition of numbers or be visited by a special bird or creature. You may witness an event, overhear parts of a conversation with important words, or run into someone who has insight and wisdom to share. Be receptive to signs and record what experience you have, as well as how you interpret them. Tonya A. Brown shared with me one of her favorite quotes from the film *Jeff Who Lives at Home* that I feel sums this up perfectly: "Everyone and everything is interconnected in this universe. Stay pure of heart and you will see the signs. Follow the signs, and you will uncover your destiny."

CLOSING PSYCHIC PRACTICES
WITH GROUNDING TECHNIQUES

Grounding is a term used to describe reconnecting with the energies of earth. It is a way of reminding your mind and spirit that you are in a physical body that is anchored to earth. Grounding is a useful exercise for closing psychic sessions and divination work, as it can help you feel more connected to your body and even make you feel secure, safe, and stable after esoteric experiences. Think of it as a closing ritual to bring you back to Planet Earth! Some people ground themselves by doing simple yoga stretches or laying down. Some enjoy a good meal or a cup of coffee. Some try a small visualization meditation.

One that works for me is as follows:

Close your eyes and envision a white light around you expanding, growing downward from your spine, and rooting into the ground.

Imagine this energy pushing deep into the ground and connecting you with the anchoring, solid energy of the earth.

If you wish, slowly bend down and place your palms on the ground as well.

While divination can be exciting and exotic, it is important to remember that divination doesn't only awe us with its abilities to foresee future events; it is also an incredible tool for spiritual development. Learning how to tap into your psychic intuition and pay attention to the gentle messages the universe sends you will not only aid you in your own spiritual evolution but inspire you to live a more enchanted, enlightened life. Messages are meant to be a support system, but your own planning and activities will manifest goals and visions.

PRACTICAL TECHNIQUES
TO REMAIN BALANCED

Some people have found that psychic work can be draining on the physical body. Psychic work and divination can make you feel tired and off balance. In addition to taking protective measures and practicing grounding techniques at the end of psychic and divination sessions, there are some practical tips for staying well that are worth mentioning. Below are some ideas for remaining balanced, alongside some questions to inspire you into beneficial practices for anyone who feels spiritual, empathic, and is working with divination.

◊ Devote daily time to meditation, prayer, or reflection.

◊ Have a dedicated sacred and magical space.

◊ Eat healthy and energizing foods. How do you feel after eating healthy foods for a few days? In contrast, how do you feel after eating unhealthy foods for a few days?

◊ Stay hydrated. What benefits have you found to keeping hydrated?

◊ Surround yourself with healthy people and imagery. What are the images, sounds, smells, and sensations that make you feel the most comfortable? What about the ones that make you feel most magical? Empaths are constantly absorbing the emotions and energies of the people around us and our surroundings. With this in mind, I highly recommend being mindful not only about who you spend your time with, but what you surround yourself with.

◊ Keep a clean space. How does a clean and organized space make you feel?

◊ Celebrate rest, relaxation, and downtime. How do you interact with rest and what does "pausing" look like in your life? In contrast to motion and activity, it is important to pay attention to when your body is seeking peace and quiet. There is no shame in rest and downtime. Celebrate motion and activity. What activities do you like to do to remind yourself that your body is a wonderful vehicle through this third dimension? Consider what activities you can participate in that allow your body to be in motion. Many people with psychic abilities work in the higher chakras, their minds and energy swirling delightfully above their bodies. By moving the body, you can return your thoughts and energy back into your present physical space while supporting the wellness of your physical body. Consider swimming, hiking, yoga, dancing, massage, sex, gardening, walking, stretching, and so on, as ways to engage with your physical self.

◊ "Be excellent to each other." How do you share love and give back charitably to the world around you? To quote time travelers Bill and Ted, kindness and charity can go a long way in bringing your mind into a compassionate space.

TIPS FOR SUCCESS WITH
YOUR DIVINATION PRACTICE

Now that we have done some groundwork for practicing divination, my hope is that you "choose your own adventure" from here. Flip through this book and find the types of divination that you are most curious about and drawn to. Before moving forward, I'd like to share with you a few tips for success with divination. These are ideas to keep in mind as you work through this book.

◊ Don't skip out on cleansing and protection rituals when you are practicing divination. While they may feel like extra steps, they are valuable methods for keeping you energetically safe. You will find that divination can lead to feeling energetically tapped out if you don't guard yourself. There have been plenty of times I've regretted not taking care to have cleansing and protective rituals after a long day of divination. Take it from me, the psychic burnout feels like an energetic hangover and is miserable.

◊ Only ask what you are willing to hear the answer to. We don't need to know everything; in fact, it may be a hindrance to know everything. Sometimes it's best to leave the future to itself and enjoy the present moment.

◊ Know your boundaries. My mantra is "When in doubt, refer out." If you read for others, you may come across someone who needs a doctor, therapist, lawyer, accountant, or other type of professional. It is okay to tell them that what they are seeking is not something you cover in a reading. Don't let them cross boundaries that make you uncomfortable.

◊ Take notes. If you are working with divination, you will find that taking notes is a great way to follow your progress. There will be a time when something happens to you and you say, "This came up in a reading I did for myself." You will be so glad you kept record of the reading somewhere to read later on when this happens.

◊ Learn about the history and culture behind the divination system you are drawn to. To show honor, reverence, and respect for the divination, take time to add notes to your studies about its history and culture.

◊ Practice with others. Find someone you feel comfortable practicing readings with. Let them know you are just in the practicing process and allow it to be a study session with plenty of notes and interaction. There are others in your community who are also interested in practicing divination together. In Nashville, we have divination shares popping up at metaphysical shops where people come to exchange readings.

CHAPTER TWO

AEROMANCY:

Air Divination

AEROMANCY IS THE DIVINATION OF READING CLOUDS, THUN-
DER, lightning, and phenomena that occur in the sky. This form
of divination is really up to the reader's discretion. Those who
practice aeromancy have personal interpretations, and the same can be
said about much of what is written in this book.

DIVINING WITH CLOUDS

If you wish to divine with the clouds, find a location where you can
lay on the ground and look up to the sky. Try to find a location where you
have a clear view of the sky above you with minimal distraction. Close
your eyes and meditate on a question that you have. Think about it in
detail, using your mind's eye to visualize the clouds moving into shapes

and symbols that will help you find resolution. Open your eyes and scan the sky for clouds, taking note of the first you see. What is the first thing that you notice about the cloud? Does it look like anything in particular to you? Use your first impressions about what the cloud looks like to help you interpret the answer to your question.

IDEAS TO CONSIDER
ABOUT CLOUD DIVINATION

◊ A cloud quickly changing its shape means the outcome will not be as expected.

◊ A cloud moving quickly across the sky could indicate travel or motion forward.

◊ A cloud that is stationary in the sky could indicate stagnancy.

◊ Dark clouds indicate a negative outcome.

◊ Bright clouds indicate a positive outcome.

◊ Sunlight breaking through the clouds indicates a breakthrough.

◊ Clouds high in the sky indicate spiritual or intellectual matters.

◊ Clouds low in the sky indicate physical or material matters.

DIVINING WITH WIND

Wind can be used as a method for telling the future and can be read by listening to the sounds it makes, its intensity, or its direction. Future events could be predicted based using the time, intensity, and direction from which wind blows as well.

On a breezy day, go outdoors and make note of the cardinal directions. Face east with a question in mind, repeating it to yourself three times. Make note of the direction the wind blows; if it blows toward the north or the west, the outcome will be positive, and if it blows toward the south or the east, the outcome will be negative.

You can also use "lots" to help you with wind divination. On a breezy day, go outside and find a flat surface on which you can draw a circle with a piece of chalk. Split the circle into four quarters, the lines pointing in the compass directions. Cut four circles out of pieces of paper and label them *love, wealth, health,* and *home.* Place them in the center of the circle and let the wind move them.

USE THE FOLLOWING TO
HELP WITH INTERPRETATIONS

◊ If a piece of paper lands in the north section of the circle, it indicates an area of abundance and wellness.

◊ If a piece of paper lands in the east section of the circle, it indicates an area that needs further research and focus.

◊ If a piece of paper lands in the south section of the circle, it indicates an area in which you need to be more adventurous and take more control.

◊ If a piece of paper lands in the west section of the circle, it indicates an area where you need to follow your intuition.

◊ Pieces of paper that stay in the center of the circle are a priority.

◊ Pieces of paper that fly out of the circle indicate that they are not a focus for the moment.

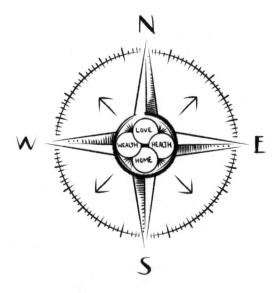

CHAPTER THREE

ASTROLOGY

ASTROLOGY MAY BE ONE OF THE MOST WELL-KNOWN, complex, and historical systems of divination. Ancient Babylonians, Egyptians, Greco-Romans, Asians, and Mesoamericans all looked to the heavens with the belief that the stars and planets above them influenced their lives and the world around them. Astrology is the observation of the celestial bodies' motion and placement throughout the sky through complex charting to interpret an individual's personality traits, determine energetic influences during a certain time period, and create predictions about events for a person and/or the world in general. What makes astrology special is that it is a system of analysis and interpretation. While you can certainly utilize your intuitive and psychic abilities in an astrological reading, your analytical abilities and interpretive knowledge will make you a profound astrologer.

In *The Complete Guide to Astrology: Understanding Yourself, Your Signs, and Your Birth Chart*, author Louise Edington offers an incredible understanding of how astrology can support our lives: "Astrology can help us live in alignment with the elements and cycles of nature, choose optimum timing for everything from farming to relationships to work life, and engage in psychological exploration of past life lessons. Astrology can help us heal our disconnection with the natural cycles of the universe and live in harmony with the cosmic cycles as they work within us," (2-3).

Astrology is a complex divination system. I have often considered astrology and tarot the more complex branches of divination, since there is a wealth of information to absorb, study, practice, and master to feel confident in using them. That shouldn't stop you from exploring them though; this just means you must be mindful that a single astrological horoscope or tarot card cannot accurately determine the outcome of significant events or explain a person.

In this section, we are going to dip our toes into the rich and vibrant world of astrology, looking at some ways you can begin studying and observing the celestial bodies and how they might influence you. Be mindful that an astrological forecast should not dictate who you are or what will happen, but that, instead, it can offer insight into how to reach your highest potential and overcome your most complex challenges.

We are specifically going to look at the building blocks of formulating an astrological analysis of a natal chart. This is basic information regarding the traits, opportunities, and potential of the astrological information that marks the time of your birth. These astrological building blocks include planets and celestial bodies, zodiac signs, and houses. You can read about your sun sign, moon sign, and rising sign in this section. If you'd like, visit an astrological site like cafeastrology.com to get a free copy of your natal chart.

Returning to *The Complete Guide to Astrology*, Louise Edington lays out the clearest way to view the difference between the planets, signs, and astrological houses by noting the planets and celestial bodies represent the "what" in your chart, the signs represent "how" the planets function in your life, and the houses represents "where" these energies take place in your life: "The 'what' in your chart represents such things as your emotions, your drive, your love nature, your mind, or to word it differently, integral parts of the self. The different signs show how those parts of the self are represented in a person and whether that is, for example, in a more enthusiastic manner or a more reserved manner. The house, or the 'where,' indicates the areas of life in which the planet and sign operate most prevalently in individuals,"(45).

ASTROLOGICAL
ELEMENTS AND MODALITIES

Let's start with the FOUR ELEMENTS and modalities that play a role in astrology. You may find the information in this section helpful if you work with tarot or are a practitioner who works with the four elements. The four elements were believed to be the foundation of life and include fire, earth, air, and water. Each element has traits and temperaments that correspond with its assigned zodiac signs. Consider which elements reign, or are missing, in your sun, moon, and rising signs, or the "three keys" (explained on page 27), which you will read more about in the section on zodiac signs.

† FIRE: The enthusiastic, energetic, and passionate element of fire corresponds to Aries, Leo, and Sagittarius. Fire signs are outgoing and take action. The element of fire celebrates expansion, empowerment, and change. Those with the element of fire are self-sufficient, outgoing, creative, and passionate. They must be mindful not to be bossy and to soothe short tempers.

† EARTH: The down-to-earth, grounded, and practical element of earth corresponds to Taurus, Virgo, and Capricorn. Earth signs have logical and dependable streaks. The element of earth celebrates organic growth, stability, and commitments. Those with the element of earth are stable, dependable, practical, and grounded. They must be mindful not to become bored or overly materialistic.

† **Air:** The thoughtful, intelligent, and interactive element of air corresponds to Gemini, Libra, and Aquarius. Air signs are driven by ideas and people. The element of air celebrates idealism, innovation, and philosophy. Those with the element of air are intelligent communicators and must be mindful not to be too indecisive or snobby.

† **Water:** The receptive, empathic, and dreamy element of water corresponds to Cancer, Scorpio, and Pisces. Water signs feel deeply and are in touch with their intuition. The element of water celebrates emotions, feelings, compassion, and intuition. Those with the element of water are sensitive and receptive and must be mindful not to become too needy or moody.

THE MODALITIES

The **MODALITIES** represent the stage of a zodiac sign within its season. There is different energy for each of the three modalities: cardinal, fixed, and mutable.

† **Cardinal:** The cardinal modality represents the signs that begin a new season: Aries marks the beginning of spring, Cancer the beginning of summer, Libra the beginning of autumn, and Capricorn the beginning of winter. The cardinal zodiac signs are all about initiation and new beginnings. They are driven and must be mindful not to be too forceful or impatient. They love to start new things and must make extra effort to complete projects.

† **Fixed:** The fixed modality represents the middle of a season: Taurus in the middle of spring, Leo the middle of summer, Scorpio the middle of fall, and Aquarius the middle of winter. The fixed zodiac signs thrive in stable and organized environments. They are determined but also need to make sure they don't become stubborn. They can concentrate and must make extra effort to honor and move through change with grace.

† **MUTABLE:** The mutable modality represents the end of a season: Gemini marks the end of spring, Virgo the end of summer, Sagittarius the end of fall, and Pisces the end of winter. The mutable modality is all about celebrating versatility and adaptability, though these signs need to make sure they stay focused and in the present moment. They are intellectual and thoughtful people and must make an effort not to grown restless or anxious.

EXERCISE

My sun sign element is ____, which means I have tendency to be ____.

My sun sign's modality is ____, which means I have an energy that is ____.

I feel most intrigued by the element ____, because ____.

THE TWELVE ZODIAC SIGNS

In this section we are going to review very brief traits of each of the twelve zodiac signs. This is a wonderful overview to give you a glimpse into the workings of each zodiac sign. For this section you will need to find out what your natal sun, moon, and ascendant signs are. There are many sites online where you can input your birth date, birth time, and birth location to calculate this.

THE "THREE KEYS": YOUR SUN, MOON, AND ASCENDANT (RISING) SIGN

In *You Were Born for This,* author Chani Nicholas explains the importance of three signs in each person's natal chart: "There are three keys in every chart that fundamentally explain your life's purpose, your physical and emotional needs, and your motivation for living" (10). These three keys are your sun sign, moon sign, and ascendant sign, which Nicholas goes on to explain: "The Sun in your chart will detail the nature of how and where you need to shine.

The Moon in your chart will tell you how you can best unpack your life's purpose daily, with great care and consideration for your unique physical and emotional needs. The sign of your Ascendant will detail the specific kind of motivation that you have for your living life" (11).

I like to think of the sun sign representing your life's purpose, the moon sign representing how you engage with yourself, and the ascendant sign as how you interact and engage with others. Your sun sign can indicate your personality and how you are motivated in life and in the outer world, while your moon sign indicates how you emotionally respond to life in your private inner world. The rising sign will show how others interpret your demeanor and character.

ARIES

ARIES is represented by the ram and is ruled by Mars. † A key phrase for Aries is "I am."

◊ When your sun is in Aries, you are a leader who is eager to push forward. You are confident, courageous, independent, and enthusiastic. You must be mindful not to come off as bossy or pushy. *Famous people with their sun in Aries include Thomas Jefferson, Mariah Carey, Lady Gaga, Ram Dass, and Leonardo da Vinci.*

◊ When your moon is in Aries, you are an engaging and proactive person who does not like to feel weak or scared. You have a competitive edge and are always willing to rise to a challenge. You are an encouraging person and do well with bold and outspoken people. You must learn to develop patience and ask others for help when you need it.

◊ When your ascendant sign is in Aries, you have strong leadership skills. You are easily excited and make a great cheerleader for friends and colleagues. You can be direct and fast moving and should be mindful that you do not need to be first in line all the time.

TAURUS

TAURUS is represented by the bull and is ruled by Venus. † Key phrases for Taurus are "I build" or "I have."

◊ When your sun is in Taurus, you are known for being grounded, determined, and patient. You are artistic in nature, enjoying the beautiful things in life. You are a dependable companion, though must be cautious not to be stubborn or argumentative. *Famous people with Taurus sun signs include William Shakespeare, Jerry Seinfeld, Robert Smith, and Stevie Wonder.*

◊ When your moon is in Taurus, you enjoy a simple and relaxing home. You like comfort, going with the flow, and having routines. You seek out things of value and do well with finances. Others enjoy your company because you are agreeable. You must learn to counteract laziness with activity.

◊ When your ascendant sign is in Taurus, you are supportive and loyal, slow and steady. You can be comforting to others and very generous. You can be excellent with business while having a splendid ability to create beauty and art. It is important to realize that you do not need to own and collect everything.

GEMINI

GEMINI is represented by the twins and is ruled by Mercury. † A key phrase for Gemini is "I think."

◊ When your sun is in Gemini, you are thoughtful, expressive, and talkative. While you may love to read and try have a variety of experiences, you must be mindful not to become scattered or restless. *Famous people with Gemini sun signs include John F. Kennedy, Marilyn Monroe, Prince, and Allen Ginsberg.*

◊ When your moon is in Gemini, you have a curious side and love to learn and read. You have a good sense of humor and need to keep mentally busy. You are articulate and do well getting messages where they need to go. You must learn how to relieve tension and calm nerves.

◊ When your rising sign is in Gemini, you are sociable, curious, and witty. You are full of questions, poetry, and stories and use them to create thought-provoking conversations. It is important for you to work on listening deeply to others and find ways to define how you can be dependable.

CANCER

CANCER is represented by the crab and is ruled by the moon. † A key phrase for Cancer is "I feel."

◊ When your sun is in Cancer, you are known to be emotional, sensitive, and nurturing. You may have a vast imagination and be a helpful companion. You might also be prone to moodiness and neediness. *Famous people with Cancer sun signs include Alexander the Great, Ernest Hemingway, Princess Diana, and Frida Kahlo.*

◊ When your moon is in Cancer, you love to nurture and comfort those close to you. Even though you have a hard exterior, you are very connected with your imagination and emotions. Sometimes you feel misunderstood by others, so you prefer the comfort and safety of home and familial company. You must learn how to venture away from home to experience the world at large.

◊ When your rising sign is in Cancer, you come off as sensitive, perhaps even shy or introvertive (and that's okay!). You are caring, affectionate, and able to make people feel comfortable. It is important for you to discover what brightens your mood and how to be as gentle with yourself as you are with others.

LEO

LEo is represented by the lion and is ruled by the sun. ✝ Key phrases for Leo are "I lead" and "I will."

◊ When your sun is in Leo, you are charming, ambitious, and active. You are known to be dramatic and proud and enjoy being in the spotlight. *Famous people with Leo sun signs include Barak Obama, Amelia Earhart, Madonna, and Alfred Hitchcock.*

◊ When your moon is in Leo, you are charismatic, generous, and inspiring. You have a love for the dramatic and theatrical. You don't need to rely on anyone but yourself, as you are very self-reliant, even though you are not as introspective as others. You must learn how to be gentler with others, recognizing that not everyone is as outgoing as you are.

◊ When your rising sign is in Leo, you love attention, are a natural performer, and remain hopefully persistent. You appear generous and optimistic, using humor and cheerfulness to brighten the world around you. It is important to ensure that you pause before you react and avoid impulsive decisions.

VIRGO

VIRGO is represented by the virgin and is ruled by Mercury. ✝ A key phrase for Virgo is "I analyze."

◊ When your sun is in Virgo, you are known for being ethical, analytical, and meticulous. While you love to be diligent with your routine and organization, it is important for you not to be hypercritical of others. *Famous Virgos include Beyoncé, Keanu Reeves, Stephen King, and Freddie Mercury.*

◊ When your moon is in Virgo, you can be analytical and like to have an orderly and organized home. You love to serve others and would make an excellent teacher. You must learn how to feel motivated through self-encouragement and not just the words or efforts of others.

◊ When your rising sign is in Virgo, you appear hard-working and likely have "pays attention to detail" on your resume. You may not be quick to reveal your feelings but will open up with time when you begin to trust the people around you. It is important for you to avoid being hypercritical of yourself and others or feel the need to micromanage.

LIBRA

LIBRA is represented by a set of scales and is ruled by Venus. ✝ A key phrase for Libra is "I balance."

◊ When your sun is in Libra, you are known for your diplomatic capabilities and are able to socialize with fairness and grace. You love poetry, culture, and art. It is important to avoid being fickle or putting others before yourself. *Famous people with Libra sun signs include John Lennon, Mahatma Gandhi, Eleanor Roosevelt, Alexandria Ocasio-Cortez, and Mickey Mantle.*

◊ When your moon is in Libra, you need to be in a peaceful and beautiful environment to feel comfortable. You see yourself as elegant and charming. You are always learning about fairness and balance. You must learn that not everyone will like you and you can be happy all on your own.

◊ When your rising sign is in Libra, you make a perfect peacemaker through your cool-kid charm and social skills. You love a good party, a good vacation, and a good conversation. It is important for you to be clear, honest, and agreeable.

SCORPIO

Scorpio is represented by the scorpion and is ruled by Pluto. † A key phrase for Scorpio is "I desire."

◊ When your sun is in Scorpio, you are known for your intensive and strategic nature. Scorpios are deep thinkers and deeply private. While they can be secretive, it is also important to avoid growing jealous or coming off as intimidating. *Famous Scorpios include Marie Antionette, Bill Gates, Adam Driver, Sylvia Plath, and Pablo Picasso.*

◊ When your moon is in Scorpio, you have an intense personality and crave deep and passionate experiences. You can be harshly honest, but you see yourself as profound and wise. You would do well to keep company with others who can handle your intensity but also lighten the mood. You must learn to forgive and forget.

◊ When your rising sign is in Scorpio, you appear intense and intimidating, perhaps even a little mystical. A word that often comes up for this placement is "magnetic" and can be extremely resourceful. It is important for you not to be too short, sarcastic, or outlandish in discussions with others.

SAGITTARIUS

Sagittarius is represented by the archer. † Key phrases for Sagittarius are "I wonder" or "I understand."

◊ When your sun is in Sagittarius, you are known for being adventurous and optimistic. They are sincere thought leaders who can be encouraging and honest with others. It is important for Sagittarians to be careful about not being too pushy or chatty. *Famous people with Sagittarius sun signs include Mark Twain, Winston Churchill, Miley Cyrus, and Frank Sinatra.*

◊ When your moon is in Sagittarius, you can be very optimistic and easygoing. You love freedom, adventure, and travel. You may have a sensitive side, even if you appear carefree and mellow. You must learn to be more mindful of how you interact with others, taking care to think before you speak.

◊ When your rising sign is in Sagittarius, you appear as the free-spirited wanderer. You are optimistic and excited to try and experience new things. You probably love to talk about your travels and will encourage others to discovering a deeper sense of self. It is important to work on avoiding impulsivity or recklessness.

CAPRICORN

CAPRICORN is represented by the sea goat. † Key phrases for the Capricorn are "I achieve" or "I use."

◊ When your sun is in Capricorn, you are known for being determined, hardworking, and resourceful. You are disciplined in nature and ambitious to "get the job done." It is important for you to be careful from withdrawing or being too critical of yourself. *Famous Capricorns include David Bowie, Elvis Presley, Martin Luther King, Jr., J.R.R. Tolkien, and Isaac Newton.*

◊ When your moon is in Capricorn, you are ambitious and need to feel recognized by others. You can become over-focused on achieving goals and would benefit from others who shift your focus to less serious tasks. You must learn to be compassionate with others.

◊ When your rising sign is in Capricorn, you are like the employee of the month or honors student. You work hard because you are goal-driven and hard-working. Others see you as dependable and prepared for anything. While you are completely loyal to those you love, you may not reveal your feelings freely and are slow to open up.

AQUARIUS

AQUARIUS is represented by the water bearer. † A key phrase for Aquarius is "I know."

◊ When your sun is in Aquarius, you are known for being unique, eccentric, and dynamic. While you may be the weirdo of the zodiac, your progressive nature can lead to intellectual breakthroughs. It is important for you to be open to others and avoid seeming aloof. *Famous people with Aquarius sun signs include Charles Darwin, Abraham Lincoln, Frederick Douglass, and Wolfgang Amadeus Mozart.*

◊ When your moon is in Aquarius, you are an individual who thrives on self-expression. You need a free-flowing environment and would benefit from being around other free spirits. You have a knack for the psychic arts and are on a search for spiritual understanding. You must learn to accept unpredictable events.

◊ When your rising sign is in Aquarius, you can be silly and quirky while simultaneously being intelligent and truthful. Your progressive and unique perspective can shed new and refreshing light onto situations and push boundaries. You love to support the disadvantaged and have a humanitarian streak. It is important for you to find focus and have rituals in place to keep you on time.

PISCES

PISCES is represented by the fish.
† A key phrase for Pisces is "I believe."

◊ When your sun is in Pisces, you are known for being sensitive and introspective. You look out for others and are compassionate and charitable in nature. It is important for you to go inward and use your spirituality and creativity to push away pessimism and soothe hurt feelings. *Famous people with their sun in Pisces include Albert Einstein, Kurt Cobain, George Washington, Elizabeth Taylor, and Steve Irwin.*

◊ When your moon is in Pisces, you are a highly sensitive person with an open heart. You are gentle and compassionate and need to be mindful to heal and rest after interacting with others. You must learn to commit to a belief or goal.

◊ When your rising sign is in Pisces, you come off as a gentle soul who gets along well with others. You can be vulnerable and sensitive, poetic and mystical. It is important to find ways to protect yourself from other people's bad motives or attitudes, as your empathic energy will take on the moods and expressions of those around you.

EXERCISE

My sun sign is ____, which means I identify as ____

and shine when I am ____.

My moon sign is ____, which means I am privately feeling ____

and am most comfortable when ____.

My rising sign is ____, which means others see me as ____

and allows me to interact to others by ____.

PLANETS AND CELESTIAL BODIES

Planets and celestial bodies (such as asteroids and dwarf planets) express different types of energies and qualities meaningful to a person's exploration of life. The movement of planets and celestial bodies through the sky can indicate what energy is occurring and how it influences a person or situation.

◊ THE SUN shows your individuality, basic identity, purpose in life, and where you want to shine.

◊ THE MOON rules over emotions, feelings, psychic impressions. As the nurturer, the moon shows what makes you feel most comfortable, in addition to your private life and internal rhythms.

◊ MERCURY rules over communication, learning, and travel. As the messenger, Mercury shows how you communicate best and your ability to think and learn.

◊ VENUS rules over the arts, beauty, love, and culture. As the lover, Venus shows you what partnerships mean to you, how you attract people, and what you enjoy in life.

◊ MARS rules over instincts, urges, work, and energy. As the warrior, Mars shows you what you are driven to accomplish and what you put most of your energy into.

◊ JUPITER rules over wealth, growth, expansion, and luck. As the sage, Jupiter shows you what you do in pursuit of truth and where you have good fortune.

◊ SATURN rules over limitations, delays, and organization. As the taskmaster, Saturn shows you what you need discipline in, where you feel limitations, and what you want more security in.

◊ URANUS rules over magic, individuality, and originality. As the revolutionary, Uranus shows you what makes your unique world and your own brand of magic.

◊ **Neptune** rules over spirituality, escapism, and mysticism. As the dreamer, Neptune shows what ascension means to you, your spiritual needs, and things you have trouble being honest with yourself about.

◊ **Pluto** rules over transformation, psychology, and the hidden world. As the transformer, Pluto shows you what areas of life have complexity.

◊ **Chiron** is a planetoid between Saturn and Uranus and is known as the "wounded healer." It represents deep wounds in your life and what needs holistic healing and tenderness in your life.

◊ **Ceres** is a dwarf planet in the asteroid belt between Mars and Jupiter. Ceres represents a nurturing mother, representing the ability to love and care for yourself and others. This placement may also show your relationship with grief.

◊ **Pallas** is an asteroid in the belt between Mars and Jupiter. Pallas represents a creative wise woman, representing how you are able to create original ideas and where you have a bright intelligence.

◊ **Vesta** is an asteroid in the belt between Mars and Jupiter. Vesta represents a virgin goddess but is also known to represent sisterhood. Vesta can show where you need to focus your energies and the ambitions you are deeply devoted to.

◊ **Juno** is an asteroid in the belt between Mars and Jupiter. Juno represents a queen or married partner and can indicate valuable relationships and marriage in your life.

THE TWELVE HOUSES

An astrology chart is a circular representation of where planets and constellations are at a given time. The natal chart maps out the sky at the exact time of your birth. The chart is split into twelve thirty-degree houses, each representing a phase in life, a type of experience, and valuable aspects of your life. When a planet is in a house, its energy is expressed in the experience or phase associated with the house.

◊ **(1) First House** rules the self, body, appearance, and identity. It is where the world sees you and the personality you give to the world.

◊ **(2) Second House** rules resources, finances, and livelihood. It is where you find value in yourself and the world around you.

◊ **(3) Third House** rules over communications, learning, information, siblings, and short trips. It is where you are collecting information and focused on awareness of the moment.

◊ **(4) Fourth House** rules over home, parents, heritage, and your roots. It is where you are privately seeking security and nurturing self-care.

◊ **(5) Fifth House** rules over romance, sex, pleasure, creativity, and children. It is where you are having fun and expressing yourself.

◊ **(6) Sixth House** rules over routines, health, habits, and work. It is where you see your day-to-day routines and duties.

◊ **(7) Seventh House** rules over significant relationships, marriage, arrangements, and partnerships. It is where you see those deep connections and what you want from others.

◊ **(8) Eighth House** rules over mental health, psychological issues, intimacy, and death. It is where you want support from others, and perhaps even your ties to the occult.

◊ **(9) Ninth House** rules over travel, education, religion, and philosophy. It is where you receive higher learning, explore spirituality, and wander the world for culture.

◊ **(10) Tenth House** rules over career, reputation, ambition, and fame. It is where your public image takes shape.

◊ **(11) Eleventh House** rules over friends, wishes, dreams, emotional ties, and networks. It is where you feel love from your community and are able to dream about your future and deepest desires.

◊ **(12) Twelfth House** rules over karmic debts, completions, spiritual devotion, and imagination. It is where you keep things hidden from others.

CHARTING THE MOON'S TRANSIT

The moon passes through our sky and transits into different astrological signs every two to three days, offering varying energies and opportunities while in each. You can follow current moon transits with an almanac or astrological calendar.

◊ **TRANSIT MOON IN ARIES:** This is a time of higher energy. Use the energy to initiate new projects and goals, such as applying for new jobs and schedule appointments.

◊ **TRANSIT MOON IN TAURUS:** This is a time of mellow energy. Use this energy to connect with nature and plan long term goals. It's an excellent time to meet with loved ones and establish romantic connections.

◊ **TRANSIT MOON IN GEMINI:** This is a time of changeable energy. Use this time to catch up on emails, phone calls, or journal entries. Have conversations with authority, make proposals, and speak your mind.

◊ **TRANSIT MOON IN CANCER:** This is a time of nurturing energy. You may feel sensitive. If you do, try a bath or restful reading session. Take care of yourself and loved ones. Practice a new form of divination during this time.

◊ **TRANSIT MOON IN LEO:** This is a time of bold and expansive energy. Treat yourself to something special like going to a concert with a good friend. Take a break from routine and do something that will be memorable.

◊ **TRANSIT MOON IN VIRGO:** This is a time of mindful energy. Focus on your health and wellness. Clean your house, eat a healthy meal, or organize your day planner.

◊ **TRANSIT MOON IN LIBRA:** This is a time of accommodating energy. Use this time to be social or make a to-do list. Start a new relationship or have a romantic encounter during this time.

◊ **TRANSIT MOON IN SCORPIO:** This is a time of intense energy. Avoid being impulsive or making passion-driven decisions. It can be a transformative time, so consider meditating or getting a divination reading.

◊ **Transit Moon in Sagittarius:** This is a time of hopeful energy. Enjoy light-hearted activities during this time. Throw a party or go out with new friends. Plan travel for yourself or try something new.

◊ **Transit Moon in Capricorn:** This is a time of ambitious energy. Resolve any looming issues and focus on making money.

◊ **Transit Moon in Aquarius:** This is a time of explorative energy. Consider what changes would bring pleasure into your life. Try some strange or inspiring new activity.

◊ **Transit Moon in Pisces:** This is a time of spiritual energy. Express yourself artistically or go on a romantic date.

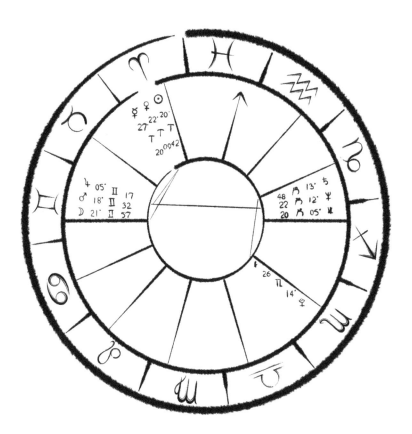

GOING DEEPER

As mentioned in the beginning of this section, astrology is a complex form of divination. While learning a few basic themes and ideas can be an inspiring springboard to better understanding yourself and others, there is always something more to learn with astrology and plenty of places to look deeper. If you are ready to take the next steps in learning astrology, I recommend further reading in the bibliography of this book (page 222). Here are a few other topics in astrology that may be good topics for additional research:

◊ ASPECTS examine the distance and angles between planets in a chart. This can give deeper and more complex interpretations of a person's personality and livelihood.

◊ TRANSITS examine the current movement of planets in the sky to create predictions.

◊ VARIATIONS OF ASTROLOGY: There are so many variations of astrology that you can spend a lifetime focusing in on a specialty. For example, you may be interested in turning your attention to astrology as practiced in a specific region or during a specific historical era. In this case, you may want to explore Chinese astrology, Vedic astrology, Hellenistic astrology, or even Mesoamerican astrology.

TALKING ABOUT ASTROLOGY
WITH SUZIE KERR WRIGHT

Suzie Kerr Wright is an astrologer, tarot card reader, certified life coach, reiki master, and psychic medium. Her masterful understanding of metaphysical things makes her an incredible resource of knowledge and one of my favorite astrology teachers. Suzie got into astrology to understand humans on a deeper level, saying it was her first love.

I asked Suzie what divination has helped her with and about the value in astrology. She answered, "We're all just a part in this vast cosmos, and someone or something else is really running this cosmic energy show. When we sync up with this power/being/whatever, we get the immense blessing of feeling ourselves in our divine light—just as we came here to be. It is a fleeting thing, but through studying divination, I have learned the secret to a magical life full of incredible moments."

Suzie gives excellent advice for those interested in taking astrology to the next step, suggesting exploring the aspects of astrology that grab your attention the most as well as seeking out teachers and mentors. She also places great importance on understanding the mechanics of charts: "Spend a couple of years really diving into your own chart—all the angles and aspects, all the possibilities you have and look at where your challenges are and why they manifest in your chart. That is the best way to learn astrology."

Suzie notes that retrograde periods are valuable to pay attention to, saying, "Retrograde periods for any planet are incredible opportunities to clean up old issues in your life and move forward with more purpose and strength." This is so valuable to keep in mind, considering how Mercury retrograde has taken on a melodramatic interpretation online. Suzie also notes that eclipses and moon phases can offer deep insight that are valuable to examine in astrology as well.

Suzie also reiterated that astrology is a deep tool, noting how many types of astrology there are. "It is brilliant for personality profiles and identifying strengths, potential, challenges—it is deeply psychological. However, you can also forecast world events: the stock market and global financial conditions, the weather, events in your own city or town, your pets, where you live, work, etc." She also gave a clue to those looking to deepen their understanding of astrology:

"It's about timing. If you know the timing and understand the language of the planets as real astrologers do, you can work with the energy flowing into your life rather than going against the tide."

CHAPTER FOUR

AURAS

AN AURA IS AN ENERGETIC FIELD THAT SURROUNDS the physical body. Auras have been described as being subtle, natural energy that the body gives off, like a psychic layer or surrounding that is unique to each person. Auras are not solely a New Age study; energy emitted from the body has been studied for centuries, as seen from ancient Sanskrit texts to saints painted with halos. In *How to See and Read the Aura*, Ted Andrews writes that auras are comprised of energies that come from the physical body, including light, electrical, heat/thermal, sound, magnetic, and electromagnetic energies.

Auras are said to surround the body, emanating outward as far as ten feet, though some claim their auras can press even farther. Auras manifest in different colors – these different colors are said to be the energies our bodies give off and can reveal our physical health, personalities, and moods. Some people see auras naturally, while others can train to see them in the right settings.

With meditation, practice, and patience, anyone can learn to read auras. We are already engaging with each other's energies, so reading auras is a chance to better connect with yourself and those around you.

MEDITATION FOR COLORFUL VISUALIZATION

It is believed that auras are connected with the energy of chakras, which radiates outward into our auric space. Whereas chakras are energy points that are situated in specific locations, auras are energy fields that radiate from the body and can change, shift, and evolve. Both are associated with colors, making them powerful visual experiences. Visual meditations can help you work in a deeply relaxed state and let you practice seeing vivid images with your mind's eye. In *Power of the Witch*, Laurie Cabot has a vivid visual meditation that allows you to not only work on seeing colors with your mind's eye and pass into a deep trance-like meditation. This meditation is called the "Crystal Countdown Meditation," a countdown from seven to one using the numbers and colors associated with each of the seven chakras.

Begin this meditation by seating yourself in a comfortable manner. Close your eyes and take a few deep breaths, paying attention only to the feeling of the breath moving in and out of your body. In your mind's eye, visualize a bright red number seven. If you need help seeing the color, imagine items that are traditionally that color, so for red you can imagine strawberries, a fire truck, or something else that reminds you what red looks like. Hold the red seven in your mind's eye for a few seconds, then allow it to disappear. Now replace the vision in your mind's eye with an orange number six. If you need to imagine the color orange, think of the orange fruit. Hold the orange six in your mind's eye for a few seconds, then allow it to disappear. Repeating this process, visualize a yellow number five. Next, visualize a green number four. Then visualize a blue number three, an indigo number two, and finally a lilac or lavender number one.

This meditation can be used to begin deeper meditations, such as guided meditations or psychic work. If you wish to continue the meditation, slowly count down from ten to one, feeling heavier and more relaxed with each number. Before I complete the meditation, I like to visualize all of my chakras spinning gently and smoothly, bright and balanced. Or, when you are finished with the meditation, slowly count from one to ten, feeling lighter, more awake and aware with each number.

SEEING AND FEELING AURAS WITH THE HANDS

Some of the first steps in working with auras can be easy and interesting solitary exercises. Take your index fingers and put them together. Stare at them for about ten to twenty seconds, keeping them together while you stare. Then slowly pull them apart. Do you see a thread of light? Do you feel a thread of energy between your two fingers? Next, try this exercise in front of a white or cream-colored piece of paper. Do you see any colors around or between the two fingers? These threads of energy are part of your aura.

Rub your hands together and move them over the different chakra points of your body. Do you get any feelings or intuitive sensations when you move over certain areas? What colors do you see? You can also try to rub your hands together and hold them up in front of a white or cream-colored wall. Stare softly at the outline of your hands and determine whether you see any light or color coming off of them, thus expanding the spectrum of your own aura that you are examining. Some people will further this exercise by standing in front of a mirror and trying to examine the aura by staring into the mirror's reflection.

LEARNING TO READ
OTHER PEOPLE'S AURAS

Seeing the auras around other people can be a fascinating study into a person's personality and mood. With a partner's permission, ask them to stand in front of a white or cream-colored wall. Make sure there is gentle lighting. Softly stare or gaze beyond your partner, as if you are looking at a point behind their head. Take your time staring—your eyes may go out of focus—and gently breathe throughout the process. You may begin to see a light cloud or haze around your partner's body—congratulations, you are seeing an aura! It may take a little time to start seeing many colors in an aura this way. Many people say they see white, yellow, and blue first, as those are apparently easier colors to pick up on. Over time and with practice, you can develop the ability to see a multitude of colors in another person's aura.

Reading auras doesn't necessarily mean just being able to see them; you may feel them as well and may have already sensed some kind of interaction with other people's auras. Do you get certain "vibes" when you are around someone? For example, do you feel inspired with certain people, while with others you feel relaxed? Have you met someone you automatically liked or automatically disliked? You may be interacting with auras already!

BENEFITS OF READING AURAS

Reading auras is an opportunity to deepen your connection with—and understanding about—yourself and the people around you. By reading your aura, you can examine your level of wellness and discover where energetic imbalances may reside; you also have the opportunity to develop your psychic abilities and bond with others while practicing reading auras. Not only can you connect to yourself and with others on a deeper level by reading auras, but you can do the same with divinity as well.

INTERPRETING AURA COLORS

Colors of auras can be interpreted to better understand a person's personality, character, or mood. There are some psychics, intuitives, and healers that believe these interpretations are too generalized; therefore, be mindful of your own intuitive feelings and interpretations of colors. Take note of the colors you see and your resulting interpretations.

† **Red:** Red can show high energy, passion, and activity. In some cases, red can show stress, aggression, and frustration. Dark red could indicate a conservative person. You may feel excited or anxious around someone with a lot of red in their aura.

† **Orange:** Orange in an aura that shows high energy, sexuality, and ambition. People with a great deal of orange in their aura can be optimistic, social, and creative. You may feel artistic and inspired around someone with a lot of orange in their aura. Orange auras can indicate being fickle and mutable in nature.

† **Yellow:** Yellow in an aura shows intellectualism. People who have yellow in their aura are focused on studying, research, and philosophy. You may feel like having deep conversations with someone who has a lot of yellow in their aura.

† **Green:** Green in an aura can indicate a phase of growth and change. Green can sometimes indicate a teacher, while blue-green can indicate a healer. Green may also show someone who is compassionate and has a strong bond with nature. You may feel comfortable and at ease around someone with a lot of green in their aura.

† **Blue:** Blue in an aura shows idealism and care. People who have blue in their aura care for those around them. Blue can show sincerity and intuition. You may feel supported, understood, and listened to when around someone with a lot of blue in their aura.

† **Pink:** Pink in an aura shows love and affection. This is a common energy to see around expecting mothers and affectionate couples. You may feel happy and hopeful around someone with a lot of pink in their aura.

† **Purple:** Purple in an aura shows spirituality. People who have purple auras are profound and engage in deeply spiritual practices. A deep purple or indigo aura can show psychic abilities. You may feel intrigued by people with purple in their aura, as if they have old souls and deep wisdom.

† **Brown:** There is less agreement on what brown means; some say brown indicates illness and imbalance, while others say it indicates being grounded

in the world. Perhaps see where brown lies in the aura and if there are other colors that surround it.

† **BLACK:** Black is not a common color to see, though some believe that a black aura can show evil, addiction, or even looming death. Many aura readers advise against believing this is the only way to read black in an aura, since it could also mean illness, exhaustion, emotional blockages, and protective boundaries. You may feel uncomfortable or uneasy around someone with black in their aura.

† **WHITE:** White can indicate the presence of spirit guardians or divine energy.

MORE INFORMATION ABOUT AURAS

◊ If an aura seems small, it could mean feeling frail, tired, or weak. It could indicate a need for self-care.

◊ If an aura seems too large, it could mean the person is influential at best and overpowering at worst.

◊ The left side of a person's aura is said to be the receptive, feminine side.

◊ The right side of a person's aura is said to be the proactive, masculine side.

◊ The brighter and more vibrant the colors in an aura, the better. If they appear dull or gloomy in color, it may indicate imbalance or challenges.

◊ The aura is shaped like an egg. When a picture of an aura is taken with a Kirlian camera, it only reveals the aura around the chest and head.

◊ The aura is said to be in different layers. Colors closer to the body indicate physical conditions, while outer layers indicate emotional and spiritual feelings. If you are interested in deepening your interpretations and studies of auras, research the seven layers of auras.

MY FAMILY'S HISTORY WITH AURAS

There is a popular story in my family about my great-grandfather Daniel being able to see auras. He apparently had the curious ability to detect when a person was about to pass over.

Our family didn't know about his ability to see them until after his son (my grandfather) died. My grandfather had serious heart surgery and was home trying to recover. Daniel went to visit him, though sadly it would be their last visit. The following day, my grandfather was rushed to the hospital—the surgery failed and he passed away.

My great-grandfather was not as shocked by the news as the rest of the family. When speaking with my aunt about this, he said, "Well, I knew that was going to be the last time I saw him alive."

My aunt was surprised by this and asked, "How did you know that?"

And my great-grandfather said, "He had a very dark cloud around his head. He had a very dark ring around his head and I knew I would never see him alive again." Having never heard the term aura, Daniel described it as a cloud or a ring surrounding a person.

My aunt was surprised and said, "You see clouds? I don't see clouds!"

This surprised my grandfather, who apparently responded by saying, "Oh, you don't?" He didn't realize that not everyone could see auras; he thought seeing clouds was a natural ability everyone had. Apparently, the auras would sometimes appear to him, but not all the time. But the darkness in the "cloud" around his son gave him the ability to correctly predict his son's passing.

Strangely enough, I have the ability to see auras as well, and just like my grandfather, I do not see them all the time. I have not yet seen a "dark cloud" around anyone. Funnily enough, I could see vibrant auras around my teachers, who often taught against white boards. I think this helped me see them clearly, and they were often yellow or green in color.

I am hoping that your family will have these types of tales as well. If you are so fortunate, take the opportunity to ask about them. They are stories that can be passed down from generation to generation, showing that all families have their own special magical abilities.

CHAPTER FIVE

AUTOMATIC WRITING

DID YOU KNOW THAT YOU CAN CHANNEL SPIRITUAL messages through writing? Automatic writing is a method of allowing channeled messages to enter through unfocused writing. In other words, automatic writing seems to just *happen*. The writer does not focus on what is being written, allowing a message (or drawing or song) to come through. It is a means of receiving messages that some say are supernatural in origin, giving messages of wisdom to those who wish to try it.

This isn't a new concept. Spiritualists in the 1800s worked with automatic writing. Some Freudian psychotherapists have even used it to help their clients explore repressed memories and deep thoughts. Surrealist artists would use automatic writing to create poetry and art through what they called "stream of consciousness," using free-form writing to wander through their ideas and impulses. One well-known modern-day automatic writer is Neale Donald Walsch, who is said to have used the technique for writing *Conversations with God*. One of my favorite mediums, Cindy Kaza, uses automatic writing on the television show *The Holzer Files*.

MESSAGES IN AUTOMATIC WRITING

There are a variety of theories for what the messages in automatic writing come from. Some people believe they are messages from spirits, while others believe guides or angels are acting as channels. Others believe that automatic writing is a glimpse at the subconscious mind or the higher self. Skeptics argue that nothing supernatural is happening in automatic writing, although those who use this technique may suggest otherwise. For many, automatic writing has been a powerful tool for self-reflection, exploration of spirituality, and creativity.

CREATING A SPACE TO WORK IN

If you are interested in automatic writing, the first thing to consider is what you wish to accomplish. Why do you want to try it? What do you hope to better understand from it? Do you have questions you want answered? Do you want it to be spiritual in nature, or are you taking a surrealist or artistic angle?

Because some believe that automatic writing is a form of channeling, it is best to begin a session by creating a protective space. You may want to draw a protective sigil, a drawn symbol said to have magical powers, on top of the paper you are going to use during the automatic writing session. You can also write something to the effect of "I use automatic writing as a means of gaining wisdom—I only speak and work with bright, benevolent, higher-energy guides." You can also protect your space using incense like frankincense or rosemary or by wearing a protective oil blend. A simple protective oil could include vetiver, rosemary, dragon's blood, or cedarwood. Create a salt circle around you, or surround your area with jet, smoky quartz, and obsidian crystals. Or you can begin with a meditation, chant, or prayer. These are mere suggestions—do what makes you feel most comfortable and secure.

HOW TO DO AUTOMATIC WRITING

Get a large sheet of paper, a blank one with no lines is best. Allow your hand to rest over the paper with the pen or pencil in position to write. Keep your mind off of the paper or what is being written, and do not try to direct what is being written. You may even want to experiment with holding the pen in your non-writing hand. Some people will actually recommend that you do not read as the writing is taking place, instead suggesting other activities like meditating, listening to music, or even watching television. Some automatic writers go into a session with questions or topics already written down. If you decide to do this, hold the questions in your mind as you work through the session to see if you receive any answers.

Automatic writing doesn't always have to happen with pen and paper! There are many automatic writers that have turned in the pen for a keyboard and the paper for a word processor. If you want to try automatic typing, prepare a space and open up a document on your computer or mobile device. I have found it most effective to close my eyes and simply begin typing. You may feel your hands move, or you may feel inclined to type certain things. Once I tried an automatic typing session after finishing an article on automatic writing, and I found that the words came to me very naturally and intuitively. My hands were just the conduit through which the message was conveyed. Many writers can relate to this feeling of having a story or image already in their mind, as if it was gifted to them in a divine manner.

AUTOMATIC ART

Automatic writing isn't limited to just words. If you are an artistic person, you may want to see what happens if you work with paints or markers. If you are musical, you may want to see what happens if you just allow your fingers to move with your instrument. Perhaps you will create mystical and powerful new songs. Allowing yourself to freely work with your medium can create the beginnings of a beautiful masterpiece. While I am no artist, nor do I usually work with automatic writing, I recall trying it when I was much younger. I took a blank sheet and allowed the pencil to move on its own. When the session felt complete, I looked at the page and, at first, thought it was a meaningless doodle. I then had the feeling to turn the page upside down, and when I did that, there was a noticeable sketch of an older bearded man in the illustration.

ART OF THE LITTLE DOTS

This doodling divination comes from Gerina Dunwich's *A Wiccan's Guide to Prophecy and Divination.* If you are right-handed, hold a pen in your left hand. If you are left-handed, hold a pen in your right hand. Close your eyes and tap the pen on a blank piece of paper for a minute or two, creating small dots. When you are done, examine the dot pattern and see if you pick up any images, words, or symbols in what you drew.

WHAT TO EXPECT
FROM AUTOMATIC WRITING

Automatic writing takes practice. Many say that when they first start, they do not see any words—just large, intelligible loops. In *Buckland's Book of Spirit Communications* Raymond Buckland writes, "Many of the messages you receive, especially at first, will seem incoherent or disconnected; almost like dreams. In fact they may be dreams," (192). Over time, however, words begin to form and take shape. Do not try to read over the message until the session is done. When the session is complete, take time to review what you see and create translations or editions if necessary. Many profound messages come through for those who stick with it.

SAMPLE OF AN
AUTOMATIC TYPING SESSION

Please note, when I typed this, there was no punctuation and some sentences did not feel finished. I am sharing with you an edited and translated edition. Some of it makes sense to me, and some of it doesn't. I hope it resonates with you.

We finally begin to see the blanket of the night sky. Even from this perspective you will move toward those who wish to create sacred dwellings and spaces for us and those beyond your realm. We are always shifting. This is always a transitional period. This means it is elective to whether you wish to evolve. Celebrate new ways and new methods of wisdom—you are the gatekeeper, you are the candlelight, you are the beacon that welcomes those and heals those and supports those in your tribe. This is a call to evolve by caring for those who need it. Yet in this passage of time, we ask you to continue to pass along the ancient wisdom, as there is value in it today. There is a reason you carry it in your DNA: it is to unite all. You carry in us the ability to fold time, to connect with other realms, to gaze from the peaks of Olympus. You see from the eyes of the gods. Breathe together with the universe now.

CHAPTER SIX

BONE AND TRINKET DIVINATION

T HROWING BONES FOR DIVINATION IS SOMETHING THAT MANY cultures have done over many centuries. The African *Hakata* bone throwing is an ancient method that uses cattle bones; the Mongolian *Shaggai* bone throwing is another ancient method that uses astragalus (ankle) bones. Ancient Romans used cube-shaped bones with markings resembling dice for divination. In South Africa, the traditional Sangomas are healers and shamans who use bones in readings that are combined with healing rituals. And in United States, two common methods of bone throwing include the hoodoo tradition, which usually uses bones from chickens or opossums, and the southern tradition, which uses a variety of bones and charms in a reading. I highly recommend exploring this further with the book *Bone, Shells, and Curios* by Michele Jackson. While there are a variety of methods for bone throwing, the thread that ties them all together is that it is essential to respect the cultures they come from and the ancestors they are tied to. As Michele Jackson notes in her book *Bones, Shells, and Curios*, "Nothing you read here, study from another book, or learn from other readers will substitute for developing a relationship with your ancestors and the spirits. Nothing will substitute for time spent doing readings for yourself and others," (8). Everyone has a different way of reading the bones, and you can use this as a starting point for exploring some of the modern ways bones are used in divination.

COLLECTING BONES

First, determine what kinds you would like to use. If you are looking to create a more extensive set, you can start COLLECTING bones from a variety of places, along with other amulets and trinkets like pieces of broken jewelry and shells or other items from nature. If you are looking to create a simpler set, you can simply collect chicken bones after various meals. There will be more information below on how to interpret extensive bone sets and regular chicken bones.

If you are collecting bones on your own, do so with respect and reverence, but also keeping in mind that if you find some in nature, they will need to be cleaned for safety. You may find that many bones you are looking for are available in hoodoo or conjure shops or from taxidermists, who will all happily share information on how the bones were collected and treated. Some people enjoy the idea of finding bones on their own in nature in an ethical way. For example, you may came across a completely clean coyote skeleton in the woods. If you are a naturalist who hikes often, be on the lookout for bones that you may want to add to your divination set.

CHARGING THE BONES

Once the bones are cleaned, you may want to consider a ceremony to CHARGE the bones and make them part of your set. A small ancestral altar would be an excellent place to charge your bones. Cleanse this unique space and set up photos of relatives and mementos of theirs. You may want to consider using Florida Water to cleanse this space. Florida is a cologne made with bergamot, orange, lavender, cinnamon, neroli, and clove oils used for purification and protection and a staple item in magical and hoodoo cabinets. Leave your ancestors an offering like tobacco, coins, or even alcohol—you can personalize the offerings based on their cultural heritage or what they loved. For example, my grandparents and their siblings loved to play cards together. So on my altar, I might also include a deck of playing cards. Be creative and respectful in your display but have fun with it as well. When the bones are ready, add them to the altar so they can connect with the power of ancestral spirits.

Bones can be charged similarly to how you would charge any other divination kit. You may want to set them up so they have incense smoke covering them. A blend of resins—sandalwood, copal, benzoin, or frankincense—would be excellent for charging new divination tools. Another thing you can do is leave them in full moonlight or even charge them in a crystal grid of moonstone, amethyst, moldavite, and lapis lazuli. Once you feel the bones have been charged, keep them in a special place—it may be best to keep them in a container in which they are protected to prevent breaking or chipping.

EXTENSIVE BONE SET READINGS

If you are interested in building your own SET OF BONES, start with a smaller set and build on it when you find the right pieces to add. Assign meanings and interpretations to each of the pieces. It may be best to use interpretations that you can easily associate with the different shapes and bones. Some people will even put markings on different bones to help them remember which are which. Here are some topics or themes to consider assigning to bones in your set:

THE CLIENT: A piece that represents the person getting the reading

FINANCES: A piece that represents money, prosperity, and material wellness

ROMANCE/RELATIONSHIPS: A piece that represents love life

HOME: A piece that represents domestic life

HEALTH: A piece that represents health and physical wellness

SPIRITUAL: A piece that represents spiritual growth or journey

PEOPLE: A piece that represent people, such as a partner, parent, friend, etc.

PROACTIVE SOLUTIONS: Pieces that represent ways the client can resolve issues, such as rest, travel, research, speaking up, magic, hard work, etc.

Though the ideas are limitless and up to your own taste, here are some ideas for additional trinkets to add to your bone set, as well as some suggested meanings:

DICE: Chance, risks, or a gamble

BUTTON: Something that needs to be "buttoned up," something that connects to things

COWRIE SHELL: Ancestral guidance

COIN: Prosperity, money

THIMBLE: Work

BUCKEYE: Health

Once you have collected your pieces of bone and assigned meanings to each one, you can practice reading with them. An easy way to read them is on a piece of fabric or small mat that you can roll out for the reading to take place; however, you can also draw a circle in the dirt to throw the bones in. Some people will divide the casting circle into four quarters. Michele Jackson suggests just this, saying that pieces in the upper half are happening in the material world, pieces in the lower half are happening in the spiritual world, pieces to the left are moving into the past, and pieces to the right are moving into the future. You may find that you assign specific areas of your divination space to specific needs, depending on the reading as well. For example, if someone has a question about money, the quarters can be how to make more money, where to save, professional advancement, and other concerns.

Toss the bones gently over the mat. Pay attention to which pieces are closest to The Client piece, as these can signify what is most important for the client to focus on presently. Examine which pieces are in which area and see if you can create a story from past to present and into the future.

SIMPLE CHICKEN-BONE READING

If you wish to throw a more simple bone set for divination, you can collect ten chicken leg bones, each about four inches in length. Cleaning chicken bones feels like a ritual, which may even appeal to you.

◊ Clean the bones of any leftover meat and fat by slow cooking them in water over the course of a day. If you are anything like me, you may keep the stock for later dishes. Scrub anything remaining off of the bones.

◊ Place them in a container with dishwashing soap and water for a day or two. Take them out, rinse them off, and allow them to air dry.

◊ Place them in a container with equal parts hydrogen peroxide and water. Allow them to sit in this solution until they are as white and bright as you would like them to be—this can take another few days but check on them daily.

◊ Rinse the bones off and bury them in salt to dry them out. Check on them a couple of times a day to see if they've dried out completely.

◊ Some people will paint a varnish over the bones to seal and preserve them. This is up to you.

◊ Mark nine of the ten bones with symbols to differentiate them from the others. Just as with the more extensive bone set, you can assign your own interpretations to the bones, using the symbols as guides to differentiate their meanings. You may want to use symbols from the zodiac, numbers, or other markers that can help you indicate which bone means what. Throw the bones in a quartered circle, as suggested above, and interpret by examining where the bones fall in the circle and which are closest (or farthest) from the others.

KIKI'S BONE AND TRINKET KIT

I have my own BONE AND TRINKET KIT that I have been building up for the past few years. While it is not my main go-to kit, I have grown deeply fond of it because there are so many different shapes and textures in it. All of the trinkets have a special meaning to me, some of them even being possessions from family members who have since passed. I associate many with the feelings I get about the place I found the item as well. A majority of the bones have been collected while on hikes or camping, and the remainder were purchased through an ethical retailer.

† PENTACLE: The pentacle represents the person getting the reading.

† GODDESS: The goddess figurine represents a female or feminine person in your life.

† CRYSTAL QUARTZ: The crystal quartz represents a male or masculine person in your life.

† COWRIE SHELL: The cowrie shell represents the presence of ancestors or a need to reconnect with your ancestry.

† WOLF: The wolf figurine represents the pack. This could be your family or tribal unit.

† SHARK TOOTH FOSSIL: The shark tooth represents the predator. While it can indicate ferocity, it can also be a warning to be careful of those who may not have your best interest at heart, those who only look out for themselves, or dangerous activities.

† ARTEMIS: This is the huntress, representing independence and self-sufficiency. This could appear to indicate a need to refamiliarize oneself with the self, to learn about those things that conjure ambition and generate energy.

† SHEELA NA GIG: Sheela Na Gig is a powerful and ancient symbol from Ireland. Her image is sensual and bold, focused on her accentuated vulva. This piece represents examination of shame, self-doubt, and self-acceptance.

† **Kuan Yin Pendant:** Quan Yin is a Buddhist goddess of compassion and empathy. This represents the need to practice both of those valuable qualities in reference to other trinkets that may be sitting near it.

† **Lilith Amulet:** This Lilith pendant represents temptation, empowerment, shape-shifting, sensuality, and confidence.

† **Deer Rib Bone:** The deer bone represents stag energy and the Green Man. It is all about the magic and power of the forest.

† **Coyote Leg Bone:** Trickster energy. The coyote bone represents having elements of surprise occur and can represent trials and tests that reveal your true character.

† **Wisdom Tooth:** Coming of age. To get this means a project or perspective is maturing. There may be growing pains.

† **Pinto Bean:** The bean represents springtime. When this appears, there is a period of growth and fertility. This is a time to plant metaphorical seeds and say yes to opportunities open to you.

† **Sunflower Seed:** The seed represents summertime. When this appears, there is growth, potential realized, and events that take place during the summer.

† **Acorn from Shenandoah:** One of my favorite places in the world is Shenandoah in Virginia. It is a place where I have taken many solitary retreats for healing and reconnecting with the natural world. As this is an acorn, this piece represents autumn. This is a time of harvest and seeing the rewards of hard work. It could also represent an event taking place in autumn.

† **Swedish Dala Horse:** This is a symbol of winter for me. It is a frozen period, much like the rune Isa. This shows that there is little growth or movement forward and instead represents an opportunity to pause and look inward.

† **Catholic Pendant:** This was my grandfather's and he was a strict Catholic. For me, this pendant represents traditions and learned rituals. In many ways it reminds me of tarot's Hierophant. When this appears,

we need to examine if what we are doing is still productive or if it is an act of habit.

† **Connecticut Mica:** Having grown up in Connecticut, I always like to have small trinkets that remind me of where I grew up. Because of this, the mica represents to me childhood, nostalgia, places of comfort, and the home. It appears in a reading when the querent must examine where they feel at home.

† **Dice:** The single die represents chance. When this appears, it is all about taking a chance and having faith that destiny will reveal its most potent wins and opportunities to you.

† **Feather:** The feather indicates momentum or the need for motion in your life. It can show where things are moving or a desire to travel and see the world.

† **Fish Backbone:** The fish backbone represents adaptability. It is about learning how to be flexible in order to create change for your success, wellness, and safety.

† **Oregon River Stone:** Going with the flow. This is about leaning into the natural flow and accepting that the easiest routes are the best routes. This can also indicate a time of movement and travel.

† **Heart:** The heart represents love, romance, and deep emotional feelings.

† **Coin:** This coin has particular value to me for a few reasons. It is an Italian lira from when my father lived in Italy, minted in 1969. It also depicts a dolphin on the coin, an animal common to Ancient Roman mythology and Italian art. I call this the "Old World Gifts" piece, as it represents wealth, prosperity, and luxury. In many ways, it reminds me of the tarot's Nine of Pentacles.

† **Alligator Claw:** The alligator claw represents good luck, where fortune will be on your side, and opportunities you need to grab at.

† **Coral Fossil with Crystal:** I am particularly fond of this piece because I found it while hiking in Tennessee. What makes it even more spectacular is that it has crystal growing in it, a testament to its age.

While I am no biologist, I believe it can be identified as a *Columnaria alveolata* species. This represents patience and shows that growth will happen but that it may take a long time, as well as the right environment and support to grow in.

† **Raccoon Molar:** Nourishment. This is all about taking care of your physical self and maintaining your physical health and wellness.

† **Bullet:** This is a bullet that my grandfather held onto from his time in World War II. For me the bullet represents conflict and battles. This could mean that there are opposing opinions, fights, arguments, and disagreements with other people. The goal is to try and find peace and diplomacy for success, but clues of resolution can be seen by what sits near the bullet.

† **Runic Amulet:** This is a shield of protection and represents needing to develop strong boundaries and build up protection. What is in need of protection depends on what it sits by.

† **Opossum Backbone:** Courage. The opossum backbone encourages practices of courage, personal power, and standing up for oneself.

† **Sea Glass:** Sea glass represents a period of purification and healing, a pause to rest and smooth the rough edges out.

† **Coral Fossil (Gray):** The gray coral fossil represents the wisdom of lifetimes and reincarnation. Think of it as collected wisdom throughout life and transformation over time.

† **Key:** The key represents access, revelations, and opening doors that were once closed. This could indicate opportunities, new perspectives, the search for wisdom, or the exploration of secrets and mysteries.

Bone and trinket throwing can take a long time to master, but starting off slowly and moving forward with reverence, practice, and patience can bring you success in a form of divination that is unique and ancient. Each reader's set is unique and imbued with personal magic, making it a powerful form of divination.

SAMPLE READING WITH TRINKET KIT

The question for this reading was "How can I best access more opportunities to lead a happier life?" The trinkets were moved from one hand to another, with the seven in the diagram falling naturally into the circle. The seven trinkets that fell were the heart, Catholic pendant, pinto bean, mica, sea glass, Sheela Na Gig pendant, and runic amulet.

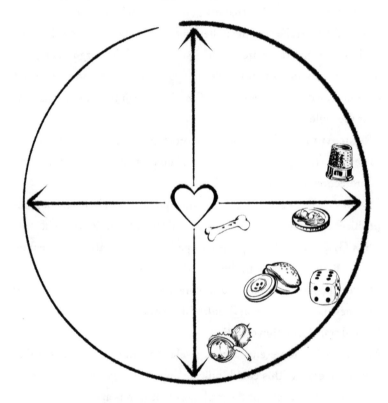

We are going to start with the heart and Catholic pendants, since they basically fell in the center of the circle. The heart is about self-love and exploring the theme of love by observing the world. It sits next to a pendant that is about traditions and rituals, so could mean that right now is a wonderful time to start regular rituals that would support the person in self-love. What is interesting is the pinto bean, lying deep in the spiritual realm, perhaps indicating that these rituals of self-love will start to really open opportunities up to the person. This may also be a time of spiritual growth.

Moving out into the future part of this reading, we see Sheela Na Gig. The self-love rituals have opened up a reflective state, perhaps a recognition that past traditions lead to a shame in need of healing and forgiveness. The runic amulet shows there is a need to protect the self—this person may be in a time where they are feeling raw and vulnerable. Part of the healing process is putting a boundary between the self and those things that are no longer working.

Moving farther out, we see the sea glass, and since it's closer to the material line, I wonder if there are both spiritual and physical needs for healing. They may go hand in hand. There may be purification rituals that need to come up, or the recognition that purification and protection are important parts of a daily ritual for self-love.

Farthest out is the piece of mica. This is a comforting conclusion to the reading, indicating being in a space of comfort. It's in a material position, so I also wonder if there is a ritual to go back to a childhood place and have a ritual of closure or forgiveness for anything that no longer serves purpose moving forward.

But to answer the question from the beginning: opportunities come from self-love, self-forgiveness, and rituals for healing, purification, and protection. These rituals may be both spiritual and physical in nature, and performing them regularly will bring balance, comfort, and happiness to the person. The pinto bean shows that opportunities are already available, and since it sits in the spiritual realm, it may be worth letting the person know that asking divinity or ancestors for assistance or a sign may be helpful.

CHAPTER SEVEN

CARTOMANCY:

Divination with Tarot, Oracle, and Lenormand

C ARTOMANCY IS DIVINATION USING CARDS. IN THIS SECTION, you'll learn about three different types of card divination techniques and insight on how to approach learning them. Much like astrology, cartomancy is a complex and thoroughly written about form of divination. You can build a library on books written about these forms of divination, so perhaps this chapter will help you feel they are more approachable and worth working with.

Tarot is one of the more complex and challenging systems of divination—I think this is in part due to its popularity and availability for many to practice and research. If tarot were an instrument, I would look at it like a grand piano: able to play a variety of genres, reveal and conjure a range of emotions, and offer gifts of creativity and wisdom to those who are willing to listen to it with an open mind and heart. If you decide you want to try tarot, Lenormand, or oracle cards, please see the appendices and recommend reading at the end of this book (page 210-229) to guide you in your next step of learning!

WHAT IS THE DIFFERENCE BETWEEN
TAROT, LENORMAND, AND ORACLE?

While TAROT has seen many evolutions and varying interpretations over time, it always follows the same formula with seventy-eight cards. The cards will usually be put in the same order (though some people switch the order of the Justice and Strength cards, or even place The High Priestess next to The Hierophant). And, even with artistic and psychic interpretation in mind, the cards will always generally have the same meanings and interpretations.

LENORMAND cards are a smaller deck and a much simpler card divination system. Each card is meant to create a sentence and give a straightforward interpretation with helpful and forward advice for the person getting the reading. You will find a very brief review of Lenormand in this section, alongside an interview with Tonya A. Brown, a phenomenal Lenormand reader.

ORACLE CARDS, on the other hand, do not have a set formula. There could be ten cards in an oracle deck or there could be fifty. Their topics, illustrations, and meanings vary from deck to deck. Therefore, the oracle deck is a unique set of cards, each with a meaning based on artist and author discretion. Many people have found that oracle cards are a little more approachable than tarot, in that they are not as multifaceted. I personally like to pull oracle cards for myself regularly. They contain helpful and motivating messages that make me feel spiritually empowered as I face my day. If you find an oracle deck that you love, see if there is an online community that also works with the same deck—this may be a useful opportunity to get assistance on readings and interpretations of the cards. The best way to become acquainted with oracle cards is by following the book that comes with it, since each is so varied and different from the next. On the other hand, I feel that tarot is a deeper dive, as it is a world where there is so much to examine and consider.

A VERY BRIEF
HISTORY OF TAROT

The Sun The Star The Moon

Tarot is a complex card system, containing seventy-eight cards in total. While the origins of tarot are not fully known, there have been suggestions that the cards came from the Middle East and made their way to Western Europe, thanks to Crusaders returning home. There are those who have suggested that tarot originated in Ancient Egypt, but there is no evidence to prove this is the case. Even more out there, some people speculate that tarot has ancient wisdom and magic embedded in its symbolism that came all the way from Atlantis. Obviously, there is no evidence to prove this, though there is something mystical and romantic to imagine such a thing.

What we can say for certain is that tarot first appears in our historical record during the Italian Renaissance, when they were created by commissioned artists for wealthy families who used them in a playing card game called Tarocchi. The game gained popularity and soon made its way to France, where in the early part of the eighteenth century the Tarot de Marseille deck was created. Later that same century, tarot began to take on esoteric significance with occultists Antoine Court de Gébelin, who speculated its ties to Egypt, and Éliphas Lévi, who incorporated elements of the Kabbalah into tarot. In the nineteenth century, the Hermetic Order of the Golden Dawn, a famous spiritual order—with alumni like William Butler Yeats, Algernon Blackwood, Aleister Crowley, Dion Fortune, and

Arthur Edward Waite—developed a deck that drew in elements of occultism, Egyptian lore, astrology, and the Kabbalah. Finally, from these came more modern decks in the twentieth century, including the Thoth and Rider-Waite-Smith decks that many contemporary tarot readers use to develop their unique interpretations from.

MYTHS ABOUT TAROT

If you are thinking about getting a tarot deck to work with, you should be mindful that there are many myths and inaccuracies that will not disappear, no matter how many times tarot readers exhaust themselves trying to debunk them.

◊ "You have to be gifted a tarot deck." There is no need to wait for someone to gift you a deck or hand down an old deck to you. I recommend you taking the time to research different decks and purchase one for yourself. While some decks are a little easier for beginning students to work with, you should always select a deck that you are most drawn toward.

◊ "Tarot is evil." Tarot, like any form of divination, is not evil. It is all about the intention you put into a reading, and if your heart is in a good place and you wish to share information in a kind, honest, and compassionate manner, then you are not doing an evil deed.

◊ "You are only a real reader if you read cards in both upright and reversed positions." Cards can be read upright and upside down (known as reversed). Some readers read reversals while others flip the card around and only look at the card in its upright position. Whether you read reversals is up to you and not a reflection of your skill at tarot. I do not read reversals in readings but love studying the difference in reversals. Some say reversals show blockages of a card's energy. Mary K. Greer has a phenomenal book on reversal meanings, going into interpretations that deal with shadow work.

◊ "You have to keep your deck wrapped in a silk cloth." This myth originated from the idea that you need to treat your tarot cards with care. If this is with a silk cloth, so be it. However, you may find that you want to store tarot in an ornate box, handmade bag, or even tucked away in its original packaging on your altar. How they are stored is entirely up to you.

◊ "You have to sleep with tarot under your pillow to activate them." I personally think this sounds incredibly uncomfortable! The ritual or practice of activating your divination kit is a personal experience and up to your discretion. I have seen people unwrap a tarot deck and start using it without a problem. However, you may want to activate a deck to exchange your energy with it. You may want to try activating it with crystals, as suggested in the introduction of this book. I brought my cards to a sacred site and had them soak up the sun there; of course, this was long after I started using the deck. You can also use reiki, or energetic work, or place the deck on an altar in the moonlight. Consider what practices you feel might "awaken" a tarot deck and develop a creative way of connecting with it.

THE BREAKDOWN OF
THE TAROT CARD DECK

The tarot is split into the MAJOR ARCANA and the MINOR ARCANA. The Major Arcana, sometimes known as the trump cards because of their winning power in Tarocchi, are usually ornately decorated cards and numbered from 0 (The Fool) to 21 (The World). These cards often signify significant events, significant lessons, archetypes, and profound belief systems.

The Minor Arcana makes up the remainder of the fifty-two cards and is further broken down into four different suits, much like what we think of when we envision a deck of cards at the casino. These four suits are commonly Wands, Cups, Pentacles, and Swords. Each of these suits represents a different element, and their interpretations are shaped around the meanings and interpretations of those elements. There are also royalty cards within the four suits—these are made to represent members of a royal court—and are comprised of a Page, Knight, Queen, and King.

TAROT CARD STUDY

If you are new to tarot and you have just gotten your first deck, take a moment to enjoy looking at each of the cards, pausing to review images, symbols, and colors you like. When you are ready, pull one card to study. What do you feel when you look at the card? Do you have intuitive feelings about what the card may mean? Do you see small details that pop out to you that feel valuable? Do you have any clair-responses while looking at the card? These are all things that you should note and meditate on while studying tarot. If you find ways to have a personal connection with the card, you will be more likely to remember what it means. Below are a few keywords, themes, and insights to support you on your journey through tarot; this is merely a glimpse: it is the trailhead on a path that winds for miles and miles.

MAJOR ARCANA

The **Major Arcana** cards are said to reveal more profound lessons, magic, and archetypes. They tend to show significant changes and transformations, so if you see many of them in a reading, it can indicate a period of personal evolution and development. Often, the Major Arcana cards can have vivid and symbolic imagery illustrated into them, so take your time reviewing the illustrations in the cards, as you may find that certain symbols stand out to you.

† (0) **The Fool** represents beginnings and new journeys. This card indicates needing to explore what your heart believes to be true. The Fool enjoys simple pleasures and encourages you to do the same. This card can also indicate needing to take a "leap of faith," know you will land on your feet.

† (I) THE MAGICIAN represents communication, teaching, inspiration, and the creative spark. This card conjures up the magical saying, "As above, so below," reminding us that our world connects to the divine heavens. The Magician indicates the need to begin a project and do what is necessary to see it through its completion.

† (II) THE HIGH PRIESTESS represents intuition, exploring the supernatural, magic, meditation, and self-awareness. She appears when it is time to go deeply inwards in search of the authentic self. This mystical card indicates a quiet, introspective phase of "soul searching," and thus, spiritual exploration.

† (III) THE EMPRESS represents creation and artistic projects, expression, sensuality, harvest, development, and self-acceptance. Often seen as a maternal figure, she reminds you to nurture yourself as you nurture others.

† (IV) THE EMPEROR represents responsibilities, logistics, guidelines, leadership, and doing what needs to be done. As a paternal figure, he promotes planning and preparation to keep things secure, stable, and organized.

† (V) THE HIEROPHANT represents spiritual initiations, religious traditions, higher education, spiritual teachings, and faith. The Hierophant can indicate a need to reflect on whether or not the traditions in your life serve your higher purpose and personal growth.

† (VI) THE LOVERS represent union, relationships, love, compassion, and vulnerability. This card celebrates a soulful connection obtained through gratitude and honesty. It can indicate needing to choose between two options.

† (VII) The Chariot represents willpower, movement forward, and reclaiming control. It can suggest needing to steer the course, deciding what the best path to the destination is. On a mundane level, it can indicate travel or moving.

† (VIII) Strength represents patience and empowerment. It suggests using gentleness and kindness as a means to success or gain. This is an encouraging card that shows braveness in the face of danger. Persistence will achieve winning results.

† (IX) The Hermit represents quietness, inner examination, philosophy, and wisdom. It could indicate a solitary phase or introvertive pause to organize thoughts and reflect on philosophical and mystical matters.

† (X) Wheel of Fortune is a card of good luck, fortune, possible travel, and taking opportunities to move onwards and upwards. When it appears, it indicates needing to have faith that destiny will be favorable.

† (XI) Justice represents seeing everything clearly, truth and honesty, justice served without bias and diplomacy. With Justice, you are invited to explore what is in balance and what is out of balance in your life.

† (XII) The Hanged Man represents sacrifice, compromise, and initiation. It often appears at a time of leaving behind the mundane and approaching things from a new perspective.

† (XIII) Death represents a metaphorical death. There is a misconception that this card indicates dying, but this is simply not the case. Instead, it indicates a significant and much-needed change, transformation, and/or metamorphosis. It is the dawn of a new day!

† (XIV) Temperance appears when it is time to pause from the world and focus on healing. The focus of this card is calmness, rehabilitation, recovery, peace, and reflection. Consider how it would feel to stop momentarily and explore how you could benefit from "doing nothing."

† (XV) The Devil represents oppression, deceit, discomfort, indulgence, and illusion. This card appears when it is time to break free from addictions, bad habits, and unhealthy situations that you feel control you.

† (XVI) The Tower shows a chaotic scene and represents destructive forces. While it can indicate a massive and challenging change, it is meant to remove obstacles and things that no longer serve you.

† (XVII) The Star represents hope, destiny, a connection to the cosmos, psychic impressions, healing, and otherworldly encounters. It is an optimistic sign of improvement and can show a divine presence supporting your spiritual growth.

† (XVIII) The Moon represents cycles, imagination, dreams, instincts versus domestication, and the subconscious world. This dreamy card can indicate depression but also a strong empathic ability.

† (XIX) The Sun represents abundance, success, optimism and positivity, good fortune, and joy. There is cause for celebration when this card appears as it shows a time free of worry.

† (XX) Judgment represents rising to a calling, seeing a sign or asking for a sign, ascension, and a time of revolution. It can represent pursuing a quest or fulfilling a mission you feel passionate about.

† (XXI) The World shows completion, satisfaction, the end of a chapter,

fullness, and wholeness. It shows someone who has an enlightened and mature view of the universe.

WANDS

WANDS correspond with the element of fire. Wands cards deal with topics associated with fire, such as creativity, passion, energy, movement and motion, and healing.

† ACE OF WANDS represents energy, new creative ideas, the "ah-ha!" moment, needing to put pen to paper, ambition, and a passion for life.

† TWO OF WANDS represents coming up with an action plan, eagerness, and contemplating where you want to go with your ideas.

† THREE OF WANDS represents energy getting pushed into a goal and exploring the world around you for inspiration. This card encourages you to keep going: your magic is working.

† FOUR OF WANDS represents success, understanding what makes you feel good, and cherishing friends. There is an opportunity for applause and celebration.

† FIVE OF WANDS represents a petty argument or a debate that will end in a draw or loss.

† SIX OF WANDS represents victory, good news, a job well done, and overcoming obstacles to obtain achievement. It is like taking a celebration lap.

† SEVEN OF WANDS represents feeling defensive, needing courage, and focusing on a prize. An attitude focused on success instead of aggression is needed for a favorable outcome.

† **EIGHT OF WANDS** is a high-octane energy card representing passion, transitions, movement, and speed. Consider what slowing down would feel like and plan for a well-needed break.

† **NINE OF WANDS** represents being on guard, needing to practice caution, and having a mindful watch of the world. This card could indicate a time of examining how strength and empowerment look and feel in your life.

† **TEN OF WANDS** represents feeling burnt out, being overwhelmed, delegating responsibilities, and being under too much pressure.

† **PAGE OF WANDS** is a young person interested in the arts. He/She/They are beginning to explore creativity. This card appears when you discover what makes you feel energized and inspired.

† **KNIGHT OF WANDS** is eager to go on adventures and gain wisdom through experience. This card appears when there is a message about your passion project. You need to focus on how ambition and confidence appear in your life.

† **QUEEN OF WANDS** is a passionate and evocative person with a dramatic streak. This card appears when it is time to devote yourself to the arts and creative projects.

† **KING OF WANDS** is a charismatic leader who is outgoing and alluring. This card appears when it is time to enjoy the social world or celebrate a matured or completed passion project.

CUPS

CUPS correspond with the element of water. Cups cards deal with topics associated with water, such as emotions, love, intuition, subconscious minds, femininity, and dreams.

† **Ace of Cups** represents hope, rejuvenation, good news in love, fertility, intuition, and good feelings. It asks you to have an "open heart."

† **Two of Cups** represent a pairing or union, passion, a budding relationship, a loving bond, and a soulful connection. This card does not always have to be romantic, as it can also indicate a vital friendship or business collaboration.

† **Three of Cups** represents a celebration with friends, support systems, ceremonies, and loving rituals. It indicates that it is a time to meet with good friends and to enjoy social time.

† **Four of Cups** represent indecision, apathy, boredom, and pickiness. It warns that if you say no to everything, you will feel stuck and isolated.

† **Five of Cups** represents regret, transition, and pessimism. This card also suggests focusing on the bigger picture instead of small losses. Do not be afraid to ask for help.

† **Six of Cups** represents reunion, childhood memories, sharing, and generosity. This card appears when there are small victories to enjoy and pleasurable moments to focus on.

† **Seven of Cups** represents imagination, fantasy, and trouble focusing. It can indicate a time where it is difficult making priorities because there are too many good choices.

† **Eight of Cups** represents reflection, changing tides, and reaching a plateau, and needing to walk away. There may be a feeling of a deeper calling elsewhere and the desire to travel for wisdom and insight.

† **Nine of Cups** is known as the "Wish Card." It indicates a wish coming true, abundance, pleasure, laughter, happiness, and good times.

† TEN OF CUPS represents a promise, hope, domestication, fulfillment, and a loving home. There is a comforting feeling of "nesting" with this card and feeling genuine support from the people you love.

† PAGE OF CUPS is a youthful person with psychic abilities – he/she/they may even be what we would call an "Indigo Child," or a special child with intuitive abilities and a unique personality. This card appears when there is a phase of emotional development or magical exploration.

† KNIGHT OF CUPS is like a "knight in shining armor." This knight brings a message of love and hope. This card encourages "following your heart" and also enjoying romance and poetry.

† QUEEN OF CUPS is a feminine, soulful, nurturing, and kindhearted person. This card appears when it is time to explore emotions and spirituality deeply.

† KING OF CUPS is a compassionate person who is emotionally mature and openly sensitive. This card indicates being mystically and emotionally intelligent.

SWORDS

SWORDS correspond with the element of air. Swords cards deal with topics associated with air, such as intellectual work, knowledge, abstract thoughts, problem-solving, planning, acting, purification, changes, and communication.

† ACE OF SWORDS represents new ideas or a new plan of attack. It suggests thinking things through carefully, using knowledge and logic to calculate the next steps.

† TWO OF SWORDS represent quieting the mind, connecting with divinity, and finding inner peace. It is a time to look inwards to understand yourself better.

† **THREE OF SWORDS** shows a difficult loss, heartbreak, or working through grief. It suggests cutting out things that no longer brings you joy.

† **FOUR OF SWORDS** shows peaceful rest and withdrawal from the world. It represents energetic healing, taking time to heal, and making quiet observations.

† **FIVE OF SWORDS** represents rumors, gossip, secrets, and defeat. This card appears when it is time to walk away from bad influences.

† **SIX OF SWORDS** represent looking for a better opportunity or situation. It appears when it is time to move "onwards and upwards" by looking for a safe space.

† **SEVEN OF SWORDS** shows a trickster figure in the act of stealing. This card appears when you need to have a strategy in place and think before acting.

† **EIGHT OF SWORDS** represents feeling trapped and feeling the need to break free. It also indicates anxiety, isolation, or negative self-talk. When this card appears, it is essential to center yourself and engage with your surroundings before panicking.

† **NINE OF SWORDS** represent anxiety, insomnia, and mental illness. It appears when it is time to face and resolve outstanding issues or problems directly.

† **TEN OF SWORDS** represents mental illness impacting physical wellness. There is a need to take time off to recuperate. Things that make you suffer or have no benefit to you should be removed from your life.

† **PAGE OF SWORDS** is a young person who is an excellent student and loves learning new topics. This card represents learning something new and beneficial. It can also represent understanding your unique communication style.

† **Knight of Swords** is a messenger in a constant state of motion. This card indicates needing to be thoughtful about your actions and communication, as they will have consequences.

† **Queen of Swords** is a strong-willed and independent person. This card sometimes indicates someone single or newly single. It can also represent seeing the truth in situations or going through significant life transitions.

† **King of Swords** is an analytical thought leader. This King is someone who has seen a lot and is now in a position of power. This card appears when there is mastery of a studied topic or being in a position of intellectual power.

PENTACLES

Pentacles correspond with the element of earth. Pentacles cards deal with topics associated with earth, such as sustenance, nature, prosperity, material gain, career, the physical body and realm, and personal growth.

† **Ace of Pentacles** can indicate a new job opportunity, potential monetary income, and feeling that success is just around the corner. This card appears when it is time to examine the theme of comfort and stability.

† **Two of Pentacles** represents juggling different projects and managing a precarious balance. There is happiness in this card when you can explore what life can offer you.

† **Three of Pentacles** represents learning valuable skills, self-development, and getting the expertise you need to get the job done.

† **Four of Pentacles** represents being closed off and being prone to selfishness and greed. This card appears when there is a need to release control.

† **Five of Pentacles** represents feeling ashamed and not using skills to the fullest extent. There can be a struggle with money, a poverty mentality, or having a feeling that you are "being left out."

† **Six of Pentacles** represents charity, asking for aid, and gift-giving/gift-receiving. It could represent an unbalanced relationship or help from someone in power.

† **Seven of Pentacles** represents patience, seeds being planted, and accepting growth over time.

† **Eight of Pentacles** shows someone deeply embedded in work represents doing what you love. It appears to encourage you not to give up, as working hard will lead to great results.

† **Nine of Pentacles** represents luxury, prosperity, success, and wealth.

† **Ten of Pentacles** shows a sacred yet familial space. This card shows a need to focus on domestic matters, estate, ancestry, heritage, generosity.

† **Page of Pentacles** is a youthful person with an inquisitive streak. He/She/That can be an intern or an apprentice. This Page appears when learning a new skill set can lead to a profitable career or new job.

† **Knight of Pentacles** is someone who pauses before taking action. This card encourages you to take inventory of your surroundings and situation and remain mindful of the functions of work and income.

† **Queen of Pentacles** appreciates the finer things in life. This queen loves a lavish environment but uses it as a healing space and support for those she loves. This card is encouraging you to share the bounty.

† KING OF PENTACLES is a stable person, a boss, or a financier. This card appears when there is a feeling of being financially stable. There is an indication of success and self-sufficiency with this card.

LENORMAND

I had always believed that LENORMAND originated in Paris, France, with the talented psychic Mademoiselle Lenormand. She was such a good reader, in fact, that she read for Napoleon. However, upon further research, Marcus Katz and Tali Goodwin in *Learning Lenormand: Traditional Fortune Telling for Modern Life*, corrected this longstanding belief. It turns out that while Mlle Lenormand was indeed a fortune teller, the cards were actually produced in a deck called the Petit Lenormand in 1850, not long after her passing. Regardless, the thirty-six-card deck is in complete contrast to tarot. While tarot is symbolic, esoteric, and lofty, Lenormand is to the point. You can read one tarot card and have a day of things to meditate on. However, you must read a combination of Lenormand cards to develop a straightforward statement.

Have a specific question in mind with Lenormand. Shuffle the cards and pull three. I repeat this, because as a tarot card reader, I found that it was easy for me to start creating symbolic interpretations like I was in an art history class while looking down at the Lenormand cards. You must combine the cards to create an answer, like building a sentence or mission statement. The most popular way to read Lenormand is The Grand Tableau; this is unique to this system as all the cards are laid out at one time, each card in the deck on display. This is usually reserved for experienced readers. While each card has a meaning here, remember it cannot be read alone but blended alongside the other cards that you pull. Here are some quick and direct meanings for each of the cards in a Lenormand deck:

1. THE RIDER: swift news, fortunate news, communication or information received

2. CLOVER: opportunities, good luck, money on the way

3. SHIP: progress, travel, a journey

4. HOUSE: domestic realm, family, shelter

5. TREE: longevity, heritage, health, endurance

6. CLOUDS: confusion, change, transition, instability, depression

7. SNAKE: temptation, challenges, sneakiness

8. COFFIN: ending, completion

9. BOUQUET: surprise, gifts, appreciation, new people

10. SCYTHE: riskiness, divisiveness, cutting, harvest

11. WHIP OR ROD: dispute, aggression, disagreement, patterns, punishment

12. BIRDS: chattiness, gossip, excited, curiosity

13. CHILD: youthfulness, trust, only the beginning, innocence, immaturity

14. FOX: cunning, cleverness, trickery, guilt, plots, career

15. BEAR: empowerment, affluence, headstrong, hibernation

16. STARS: idealism, dreaming, hope, creation, blessings, fate

17. STORKS: change, delivery, faith, new beginnings

18. DOG: loyalty, friendship, trustworthy companion

19. TOWER: careful watch, space of defense, vision, ambition, isolation, authority

20. GARDEN: communing, society, networking

21. MOUNTAIN: obstacle, detour, challenges, high goals

22. CROSSROAD: choice, decisions, problem solving

23. MICE: productivity, loss, distraction

24. HEART: love, unions, attraction

25. **Ring:** continuity, proposal, commitment, pledge

26. **Book:** knowledge, learning, secrets

27. **Letter:** written word, messages, contracts, meaningful communication

28. **Man:** can be the significator, person getting the reading, or a person in the querent's life

29. **Woman:** can be the significator, person getting the reading, or a person in the querent's life

30. **Lily:** virtues, purity, sex, maturity

31. **Sun:** success, luck, optimism

32. **Moon:** dreams, creativity, fame

33. **Key:** access, discovery, security

34. **Fish:** money, resources, options

35. **Anchor:** standstill, hope, stuck in place, unable to move forward

36. **Cross:** restrictions, challenges, anxiety, suffering

TALKING ABOUT
LENORMAND WITH TONYA A. BROWN

I am so thankful to know Tonya and to have been able to work closely with her through *Witch Way Magazine* and *The Witch Daily Show* podcast. Tonya is an incredible resource for the modern witchcraft community, providing expertise and support through her book, magazine, and podcast. I have always depended on Tonya's wisdom about the Lenormand, as it is one of her go-to forms of divination, having been a reader of Lenormand for many years.

Tonya discovered this form of divination in her teens and started to work with Lenormand in her early twenties. She loved how clear and concise Lenormand was, how it felt different from tarot: "It was so clear and concise. It was straightforward and honest. The system itself is structured in a way that tarot is not and contains less fluidity. This takes a lot of the endless interpretation out of the cards. Lenormand decks are very moldable to their readers and a fast connection is often reached. While I've toyed with other decks, I am unable to reach the accuracy, ease, and clarity I do with Lenormand."

For Tonya, Lenormand readings do not need to be up for debate. Instead of each card offering deep interpretations like tarot, she reflects on Lenormand being straight to the point: "It's right there in front of you. You can't try to skate around a situation or skew the meaning. Lenormand doesn't allow that. You have to face the truth with Lenormand."

This very fact has helped Tonya feel confident with giving divination readings: "I've been reading my same deck for almost seven years now and we work together so seamlessly. The deck knows what cards to show me to get me the information. I never need to second guess. As a wand is an extension of one's arm, Lenormand is an extension of my intuition. We are one. I often lacked confidence in my tarot readings, but Lenormand has my back. It's not going to give me falsities, it's taught me confidence." If you are interested in learning Lenormand, Tonya encourages you to find a deck that you feel drawn to, just as she did, and start practicing. "It will become your best friend, your second in command. If you honor the system and honor the cards for what they are and what they do and develop a true respect for them, they won't let you down."

You may find that you fall in love the symbols of the Lenormand, just as Tonya has. Over time she has learned how the cards work with each other: "Multiple cards in Lenormand parallel each other—the Scythe and the Coffin, for example. Both mean an end. One, however means a forever end, while one means an end that will to bring new things. Sometimes that small difference means all the world to a querent. It is a fully developed and respected system. Lenormand is not a one-off oracle deck. It is an old, fine-tuned system, and if you are willing to respect the cards and respect the system, they are the most accurate cards you will ever encounter."

CHAPTER EIGHT

DICE DIVINATION

ROLLING THE DICE ISN'T JUST FOR DUNGEONS & Dragons. Dice can be a fun form of divination as well, and it just so happens to be one that you can play with to create interpretations that fit your own needs. Just like any other form of casting lots, you throw dice to receive a divination reading. Dice allow you to interpret the number you roll provide answers to your questions. Let's give the dice a roll and take a gamble to see what is in store for our futures.

DIVINATION WITH ONE DIE

Roll one die. If the outcome is an odd number, the answer is positive. If the outcome is an even number, the answer is negative. You can also use a single die to determine timing. If the outcome is one, do act on your question immediately. The increase in the number can indicate an increase in the time you should take to act upon your question.

DIVINATION WITH TWO DICE

The interesting thing about the dice readings is that the interpretations vary from source to source, making the practice feel a little more flexible for you to add your own input. The dice interpretations I offer here combine Clifford A. Pickover's interpretations from *Dreaming the Future* with my own personal interpretations, which are inspired by numerology.

1. A positive answer. A time of beginnings, new projects and a need to keep focused.
2. An uncertain or inconclusive answer. Focus on balance, partnerships, and relationships.
3. Success, expansion, and a time to be creative. Remain considerate and conscientious for best results.
4. Be thoughtful and organized to keep stability and order in your life.
5. This is a time of good fortune and success. You can take risks and be adventurous.
6. This is a gentle and easy time where your focus can be on love and harmony. Listen and support others.
7. Don't lose focus now: what you study and contemplate will lead to wisdom and mystical experiences.
8. If you are patient you will be rewarded with power, abundance, and expansion.
9. Inspiration leads to success in business and entrepreneurial pursuits. This is a good time for change.
10. This is a time of ending and disappointment. There may be unexpected endings which will lead to starting over.
11. Optimism and hope are needed to steer you towards a better outcome.
12. This is a challenging answer, showing a negative outcome and a need to change the path you are on.

DIVINATION WITH THREE DICE

In *Buckland's Book of Gypsy Magic*, Raymond Buckland suggests dice divination using three dice. Create a chalk circle that is twelve inches in diameter. Roll the three dice, disregarding any that roll outside the circle. Use the following interpretations for the number you roll (Buckland's interpretations for each number feel antiquated, so I added additional, more modern meanings for each of the numbers as well):

1. Loneliness or loss.
   ‡ Additional meanings: Solitary work, alone time, a time of introversion
2. Love or infatuation.
   ‡ Additional meanings: A relationship, romance, lust, falling in love with someone or something
3. A pleasant surprise on the way.
   ‡ Additional meanings: A pleasant outcome, a turn toward better luck
4. An unpleasant surprise on the way.
   ‡ Additional meanings: An unpleasant outcome, a turn toward challenging times
5. An influential stranger will come into your life.
   ‡ Additional meanings: Seeking out teachers, looking for lessons in interactions with others, considering how others influence you
6. You will lose something valuable.
   ‡ Additional meanings: A lost object, the end of something
7. You will be involved in a scandal.
   ‡ Additional meanings: Gossip or distrust
8. A past wrong will catch up with you.
   ‡ Additional meanings: Karmic cycles, lessons learned, someone from the past will reappear

9. A future wedding.
   ‡ Additional meanings: Partnerships, getting closer to someone, a relationship solidifies
10. Business advancement.
    ‡ Additional meanings: Abundance, prosperity, business growth
11. There will be a death close to you.
    ‡ Additional meanings: Transitory times, a need to check in with those you love, a loss
12. You will receive an important letter.
    ‡ Additional meanings: Communication that will change your outlook on things, a need to speak up but also to listen carefully
13. There will be cause for you to weep.
    ‡ Additional meanings: A time of release, a time of stress, a need to relieve anxiety or sadness
14. A new admirer.
    ‡ Additional meanings: New people coming into your life, center of attention
15. Be cautious, trouble is near.
    ‡ Additional meanings: Now is not a time to react. Take things slowly. Be careful with yourself and others. Do not take risks.
16. A happy journey.
    ‡ Additional meanings: A need to travel or move, a time of evolution or self-discovery
17. Profitable business comes to you from across the water.
    ‡ Additional meanings: There is a need to expand your horizons, think bigger, or go global
18. Great good is coming to you.
    ‡ Additional meanings: Success, blessings, and luck are on your side

ALPHABET DICE – AKA "SPIRIT DICE"

Tonya A. Brown, editor of *Witch Way Magazine* and host of *The Witch Daily Podcast*, watched a horror movie during the 2016 Halloween season in which one of the characters used dice with letters on it to communicate with spirits. This sparked a great idea to get sets of alphabet dice and attempt divination with them. I was excited when I got my own set of lettered dice in the mail, eager to try to create different methods of using dice for divination. If you are creative, you can always make your own dice using small wooden cubes and paint, both of which can be found at your local hobby shop. Otherwise, you can order two sets of alphabet dice from American Traditions like I did.

The eight dice had the following letter configurations in our manufactured set:

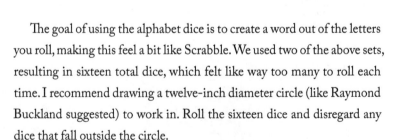

Die 1:   A, E, I, O, U, * (for wild card pick)

Die 2:   A, E, I, O, U, Y

Die 3:   M, R, H, G, L, S

Die 4:   D, C, N, B, P, R

Die 5:   W, T, M, E, L, F

Die 6:   P, C, B, D, G, F

Die 7:   W, S, H, Y, N, T

Die 8:   Q, Z, X, J, K, V

The goal of using the alphabet dice is to create a word out of the letters you roll, making this feel a bit like Scrabble. We used two of the above sets, resulting in sixteen total dice, which felt like way too many to roll each time. I recommend drawing a twelve-inch diameter circle (like Raymond Buckland suggested) to work in. Roll the sixteen dice and disregard any dice that fall outside the circle.

Place all the dice into a bag that you can easily get your hands into. First, think about a question you would like to ask. What you will want to do is first think about a question that you have. Ask yourself the question and reach into the bag to collect however many dice you feel drawn to take out, then roll them into the circle. Whatever upright letters are remaining should be examined and deciphered. See how many words you can make from the letters you have. There may be the name of a place or person. Interestingly, when I tried this method, I rolled five dice and got the letters C, O, L, D, E. Perhaps you will see words that exclude one or two of the dice, and that is okay. Use your intuition to help you determine the answer in the dice.

Another method with the lettered dice that you may want to try is to select letters that represent different options. Here is a "yes or no" method: use the die with Y for "yes," the die with * for "maybe," and the die with N for "no." Ask a question with a "yes" or "no" answer, and roll the dice until you get a Y, N, or * for your answer. Here is another option: use a die with A for "option A," a die with B for "option B," the die with * for "either option," and the die with Z for "neither option." Roll the four dice until you roll A, B, *, or Z to get your answer.

Working with the alphabet dice may seem a little complicated, but it could be a very interesting thing to try. However, you want to encounter the dice, find a method that feels right to you and get rolling.

CHAPTER NINE

DOWSING
WITH RODS
AND PENDULUMS

OWSING USES INSTRUMENTS TO HELP GUIDE A PERSON to an intended object, energy, or location to detect things beyond our human senses. You can follow the motions of dowsing instruments to be directed to specific locations, or you can observe the motions of the dowsing instruments to decipher answers to questions and inquiries. Chances are, you probably already know what dowsing rods are. Have you ever seen old illustrations of farmers holding up a Y-shaped piece of wood in hopes of finding water? That is one example of dowsing.

It turns out dowsing has quite an extensive history. There is an Algerian cave painting dating to 6000 BCE that shows a man holding a forked stick, and there are also Ancient Egyptian paintings that depict dowsing as well. A French priest named Abbe Bouly used dowsing to find unexploded shells on war-torn ground during World War I. Treasure hunter Dan Blankenship used dowsing to find digging sites on the famous Oak Island. Now, there are even societies in both North America and the United Kingdom for professional dowsers. Many people have found metal veins, precious gems, water, and even oil by dowsing.

While dowsing has been used to assist people materialistically, many in the metaphysical community use dowsing to connect with ley lines, which are energetic lines said to grid the earth and believed to connect sacred or spiritually charged places. Dowsing can help find natural paths of energy in sacred spaces or even paranormal hotspots in haunted locations. Healers even use dowsing to navigate energy going through a person's body. Learning how to dowse can help you feel more confident in your intuitive hits and get acquainted with popular techniques. Dowsing is most commonly performed with one of two types of instruments: dowsing rods or pendulums.

In general, dowsing is done with either wooden sticks like farmers traditionally used or with L-shaped metal rods. For the sake of reviewing one commonly used method, we will work with two metal rods in my explanation of dowsing. It has been suggested that copper rods are the best to use, since copper is a natural conduit for energy. Crafty people may find it easiest to go to a hardware store to get copper wire and make their own set of dowsing rods. I, on the other hand, purchased mine online a decade ago, and they still work just fine.

Take the rods and hold them firmly in your hands—employ the "Goldilocks Rule"—don't hold them too tightly nor too loosely. Keep your elbows to your sides in order to keep the rods steady in front of you. Hold the rods straight ahead, about nine inches to one foot apart from one another and parallel to each other. Focus on what it is you are looking for: Are you looking for energetic ley lines? Paranormal activity? Veins of gold? Lost keys? Whatever it is, walk forward slowly, keeping your thoughts on what it is you are looking for. The dowsing rods will cross one another when they detect what it is you are looking for.

I personally have really enjoyed taking dowsing rods with me on my travels. I have been fortunate to be able to visit many sacred destinations, and using the dowsing rods at those sites has been an interesting way to see where energy is the most profound and powerful. One place in particular that I found surprisingly magical was the Cahokia Mounds in Indiana, where we used the dowsing rods to move to different places across the site. The dowsing rods also came in handy while exploring Caracol in Belize. They crossed frequently throughout the site, but most notably at the center of the highest courtyard on the tallest pyramid in the complex. You may find that the dowsing rods lead you on a journey to find the natural and sacred flow of energy wherever you are using them.

PENDULUMS

A pendulum is a weighted object on the end of a string and is commonly used as a tool in dowsing. They are also a lot of fun to try! While traditional pendulums were needles on a long thread, today there are often more visually appealing, made with crystals that hang from light metal chains. Some people will also use an amulet on the end of a necklace as a functional pendulum. Pendulums sway to give their answers and are generally used to answer simple "yes" or "no" questions by observing the way the pendulum moves. But, as you will discover, pendulums can go above and beyond this simple method of divination.

HOW TO USE A PENDULUM

Take the end of the thread or chain of the pendulum and hold it between your thumb and forefinger. Some people will loop the chain over the top of the forefinger, whereas other will not. How you let it fall is up to you. Practice holding it in a variety of ways to see what is best for you. Rest your elbow on a solid surface like a tabletop, so the pendulum has less of a chance to move or sway on its own. Once you are in a comfortable position and the pendulum is not swaying, you can begin your session.

Take a few deep breaths and try to clear your mind of passing thoughts. Ask the pendulum to show you "yes." The pendulum will start swinging a certain way. Make note of the direction it moves. Then ask the pendulum to show you "no." The pendulum will likely start to swing in the opposite direction. For example, the pendulum may swing from left to right to answer "yes" but will swing up and down to answer "no." Or it may swing in a clockwise circle to answer "yes" and will swing counterclockwise for "no." You may also want to ask the pendulum to show you "I don't know." It's up to you. I speak aloud when I do this, but some practitioners will ask the questions in their mind. Again, try different methods, do what feels right and safe, and do what is best for you.

To test your pendulum, you can ask a question or declare a statement that you already know the answer to, such as "I am twenty-five years old" or "Do I live in Seattle?" See if the pendulum answers correctly. If it doesn't, you may want to clean your pendulum or try another pendulum.

WHAT TO USE A PENDULUM FOR

There are many ways to use a pendulum, and you may find a method that works best for you. I personally like to use the "yes" or "no" method to answer questions—this actually works well when used during tarot readings. Here is a list of ways that pendulums can be used:

† Use a pendulum with food and vitamins. Please note, the best way to find out which food and supplements are best for you is by consulting a doctor or nutritionist. Additionally, many people avoid using divination more generally as guidance, especially for others, regarding health. That being said, others have used pendulums over food and vitamins to determine whether they would be beneficial to their health. Hold the pendulum

over a food or vitamin and ask, "Is this going to be a positive influence on my health and body?"

† Use a pendulum for reiki. If you are a reiki practitioner, you can use a pendulum to show where a session should focus. Slowly move the pendulum along the energetic centers. The pendulum will hold a neutral position until it finds an area where reiki work should be done.

† Use a pendulum to balance chakras. Ask the pendulum to help balance chakras. Start by holding the pendulum over the root chakra and ask the pendulum to move as it wishes to bring balance to that area. Once the pendulum returns to a neutral position, the chakra is balanced. If it continues to move, allow it to come to a halt naturally.

† Use a pendulum with a map or alphabet board. Some people have used pendulums over maps to find locations. I had one student use a map of the city they lived in to ask what neighborhood they should move to. People have also used alphabet boards with pendulums to spell out answers. In this case, hold the pendulum over an alphabet board and ask, "Can you work with this pendulum board?" The pendulum should swing to letters or numbers to spell out a specific answer.

† Use a pendulum to help find lost objects. I have personally never had any luck with this, but perhaps you will. Play the "hot or cold" game with the pendulum. Focus your thoughts on what the lost object looks and feels like. Move slowly around a room, asking the pendulum to indicate if you are closer to ("hot") or farther from ("cold") the object.

CHAPTER TEN

FIRE DIVINATION

G AZING INTO THE FLICKERING FLAMES OF A FIRE, feeling and sensing omens in the dancing tendrils of incense smoke, and deciphering messages in the shapes of melted wax are a few of the ways that the element of fire is used in divination.

SCRYING WITH FIRE

One simple method of divination by fire is SCRYING. Scrying is divination by gazing, commonly associated with (but not limited to) crystal balls or dark reflective mirrors. Scryers will often gaze into a reflective surface with the intention of seeing divinatory messages. Fire scrying can be a relaxing exercise. Before your scrying session, consider which questions you'd like to gain insight into. Rest comfortably by the fire and gaze into its glowing embers, allowing your focus to soften, maybe even letting your vision go blurry. If your thoughts wander, try to return your attention to your breath and the motion of the fire. You may feel an intuitive answer to your question or see shapes in the embers that contain symbolic messages.

There are different ways to interpret the condition of the flames to divine future events as well. Have a question in mind prior to lighting the fire, then interpret the way the fire lights and the flames move. It is difficult to find any standard list of flame interpretations, and many sources only contain brief passages on the topic. Scott Cunningham suggests many flame interpretations in *Earth Power*:

◊ It is a good sign if the wood catches on fire and burns quickly.

◊ If it is difficult to get a fire going, the answer is not as optimistic for the moment and needs to be returned to later.

◊ Love and romance are omens if the fire moves to one side of the fire pit.

◊ Difficulties and challenges will follow if the fire crackles frequently.

◊ There is important news ahead if sparks fly into the air.

DIVINING SMOKE

If gazing into a flame is not something of interest, there are two methods of interpreting the smoke of a fire as well—CAPNOMANCY is the divination of interpreting the smoke from a fire. The direction of the smoke is said to determine the outcome of future events. In general, it is believed that if the smoke rises straight up and reaches high before dissipating, it is a good sign. On the other hand, if the smoke lingers low and near the fire, it is not as fortunate an omen.

If you are interested in trying something on a smaller scale, you can do as the Babylonians did and divine with incense smoke—LIBANOMANCY is the divination of smoke from incense. There are ancient Babylonian texts that describe how incense smoke was used to predict outcomes of battles and confrontations. While ancient interpretations are challenging to modernize for today's diviners, especially with passages like this one: "If the top of the incense gathers like a date palm and is thin at its base hardship will seize the man."

Here are some suggestions for libanomancy interpretations to try:

◊ If the smoke comes toward you, the answer is "yes."

◊ If the smoke moves away from you, the answer is "no."

◊ If there is a lot of smoke, you will have abundance and success.

◊ If the incense goes out, you will have to wait longer to see results.

OBJECTS IN THE FIRE

An ancient method for conjuring messages from fire divination includes throwing objects onto the fire. ALOMANCY, sometimes known as HALOMANCY, is divination involving throwing salt into the fire. The sounds of the fire, as well as the color of the flame, would then be interpreted. DAPHNOMANCY is the divination of throwing bay laurel leaves onto a fire. If you'd like to try this, hold a bay leaf with a question in mind, then throw the leaf into the fire. The louder the crackling of the bay leaf burning, the more optimistic the outcome of your question.

Nuts have also been thrown into fires to give answers. In Wales, there was a New Year's bonfire tradition associated with nuts. Throw a nut into the flames of a bonfire, and if the flames dance when the nut is thrown in, it will be an exciting, fun year. If the flames do not change when the nut is thrown in, it will be a dull year.

CANDLE DIVINATION

PYROMANCY can be performed with candles as well, and there are different methods that can be used with a simple spell candle to look for future omens. Candle divination examines the condition of the flame and the shape of the wax for prophetic interpretations. You can use the following list as guidance for scrying with a candle flame:

◊ The higher and brighter a flame burns, the better the outcome.

◊ If the wick leans toward you, the outcome is "yes."

◊ If the wick leans away from you, the outcome is "no."

◊ A flickering flame indicates change is on the way.

◊ A sparking flame indicates possible challenges.

◊ If wax drips to the left side, the answer is "no."

◊ If wax drips to the right side, the answer is "yes."

◊ If wax drips equally on both sides, there is no response.

◊ If there is no wax dripping down the sides of the candle, ask again later.

Ceromancy is the divination of wax shapes. Light a candle and let it burn until there is melted wax collecting. Carefully pour the wax into a bowl of cold water, then take the wax out and interpret its shape. Interpreting wax shapes can feel similar to interpreting tea leaves and are often dependent on the reader and their interpretation of the shapes depicted in the wax. It may be worthwhile to note the shapes you see and follow up with the querent to see what outcomes follow the reading. It may also be worthwhile to cross reference glossaries for the meanings of shapes in tea-leaf readings. Perhaps a heart would represent love, or a coin would represent prosperity. If you see a baby, it could mean new beginnings. Or, if you see an animal, it may be worth exploring the meanings of its spirit.

SPODOMANCY

One interesting, curious divination technique discussed by Courtney Weber in her book, *Brigid: History, Mystery, and Magick of the Celtic Goddess*, is SPODOMANCY, or divination with ashes to try on Imbolc, the holiday which honors the Goddess Brigid and celebrates the first signs of light and warmth returning to the world. She suggests that you smooth out the ashes and soot in your fireplace before bed on Imbolc eve. Check on the ashes the following morning. If they look as if they have been disturbed or have footprints in them, then Brigid came to visit and bless your home during the night. Another way to read ashes can be done as follows. Spread out ashes in an area that is exposed to a breeze. Perhaps you have a stone you can spread them across or a tray you can put near an outdoor altar, or you can use a porch that you don't mind sweeping. Write a question you have in the ash and allow it to sit overnight. Whatever letters are legible the following morning can be deciphered and interpreted to show the answer to your question.

You can also try pyromancy, the divination method described above, and Imbolc is a wonderful time to cozy up with the element of fire. It may take time to understand the messages or come up with your own interpretations, but it is worth the effort of working with such a relaxing and ancient form of divination.

CHAPTER ELEVEN

FOOD DIVINATION

HOMEBODIES AND KITCHEN WITCHES, UNITE! THERE ARE SO many varieties of divination that take place in the kitchen. Some are more peculiar than others, and some can easily be done while cooking, whereas others require a little more preparation.

DIVINING OF EGGS

EGG DIVINATION has long been practiced, and at times in history, it was a popular form of divination. While some methods are easier than others, and some are neater than others, they are all fun to experiment with.

† OOMANCY: Oomancy is divining with the egg white. Bring a pot of water to boil, then lower the heat slightly. Break an egg and separate the white from the yolk. Pour the egg white into the boiling water and interpret the shapes they make. When divining the shapes, consider your immediate reaction to what you see.

† OOMANTIA: Oomantia is divining with the eggshell. An excellent egg divination described by Nancy Vedder-Shults in her article "Egg Divinations" suggests to hard boil an egg. Draw different symbols on the egg, giving meaning and interpretation to each of the symbols. Hold the egg

and think of your question, then gently roll the egg. When it stops rolling, your answer can be found in the symbol facing upward. Another method for reading eggshells includes cracking a hardboiled egg and interpreting the shapes and lines made with the cracks in the shell.

† Ooscopy: A fun, yet messy form of egg divination that involves reading the shell, white, and yolk, ooscopy is the divination of the whole egg. Hold an egg for a moment and concentrate on a question you have. Throw the egg onto the ground, or perhaps in a dish, and interpret the shapes of the egg and shell to come to a divine answer.

† Egg Superstitions and Old Traditions: There is an old tradition that says you will have a lousy day if you crack an egg at breakfast and break the yolk. Cracking an egg with a double yolk is usually a good sign, often signifying a pregnancy or happy union; unless you are British, in which case a double yolk is a sign of death or ill fortune. An old Scottish divination suggests filling your mouth with the white of an egg, not swallowing a drop. You are to then go out and about in the world until you hear the name of a man or woman. This is the name of the person you will marry.

DIVINATION OF WINE

Did you know that you can combine the pleasure of a glass of wine with scrying? Oinomancy is divination using wine. Pour a glass of red wine into a clear glass and place a candle behind the glass. Sitting in front of the glass, gaze into the illuminated wine to scry and search for symbols and omens. Another potential way to divine wine is to read the residue left in the bottom of the glass, or read the way the wine swirls, splashes, and moves against the side of the glass.

DIVINATION OF CHEESE

Tiromancy, the divination of cheese, was apparently saw a peak in popularity during the Middle Ages. The shape of the holes in cheese were interpreted; for example, a heart shape would indicate love, and letters would be sought to indicate initials. The aging process of cheese may have been read, as well as the quantity and shapes of mold. One other method with cheese that may have been used was to assign slices of cheese to specific people or outcomes. The cheese would then be fed to rodents, and the first piece to be eaten entirely would indicate the answer. Since it was rather wasteful to let a good Brie turn moldy—or a little gross to collect rodents for cheese-eating races—tiromancy eventually lost its popularity to other forms of divination. Perhaps you will feel adventurous enough to divine the shapes of the holes in a slice of Swiss or create a new method altogether for reading cheese. Maybe forego the rats, though.

DIVINATION OF SALT AND FLOUR

HALOMANCY is the divination of salt and the patterns it makes after being poured onto a surface. To try this method, you will need coarse sea salt and a tray or dish that you can pour salt onto. Take a small handful of salt and consider a question you have in mind. Pour it onto the surface and interpret the shapes the salt makes. If the salt goes toward the right of the dish, there will be progress forward and growth in your near future. If the salt stays mostly to the left of the dish, there will be transition or change in the near future. A large mound or pile of salt indicates obstacles, while round shapes or circles indicate money. Lines indicate traction forward or travel.

You may also wish to pour an even layer of fine salt onto a dish or tray. Close your eyes and allow your finger to draw freely in the surface. Interpret the shapes and designs you drew in the salt. A variation of this is to throw a handful of salt into a fire. Interpret the future based on the sounds you hear from the fire, as well as any shapes you see in the fire resulting from the salt.

ALEUROMANCY is the divination of flour and is linked to the fantastic fortune cookie. In Ancient Greece, priests would write wise and inspiring messages on small pieces of paper that were baked into cakes. Another method of divining with flour would be to interpret shapes in a water mixture. Mix flour and water in a bowl and interpret the shapes that the mixture takes.

DIVINATION OF
FRUITS AND VEGETABLES

The produce section also offers an array of oracular options. For example, you can use an orange to receive a simple "yes" or "no" answer. While eating an orange, consider a question you would like answered, saving all the seeds. Count the number of seeds in the orange—an even number means the answer is "no," and an odd number means the answer is "yes." Cromniomancy is the divination of onions. One method of reading onions involves carving the initials of potential suitors into the onion skins. The first onion to sprout would be the chosen love. There is even a woman in England who calls herself an "Asparamancer," as she casts a bundle of asparagus stalks and interprets the patterns they form when they land.

There are numerous forms of divination associated with apples, which were commonly practiced as party games for Halloween in the Victorian era to determine a person's romantic future. Keep in mind that these are old, traditional forms of divination from different times. They may need a little modification for our modern world, and that is okay to do in your own practice. Here are some different ways to use apples in divination:

Cut an apple in half and count the seeds. Two seeds indicate an early marriage. Three seeds indicate inheritance. Four seeds indicate wealth and prosperity. Five seeds indicate travel. Six seeds indicate fame as a speaker, actor, or singer. Seven seeds indicate dreams and wishes to be fulfilled. Another variation using apple seeds to predict a romantic future suggests that an even number of seeds indicates a partnership in the near future, whereas an odd number of seeds indicates you will remain single for the time being. If a seed was cut from slicing the apple, any potential romantic relationship could be tumultuous.

This is traditionally done on Halloween, though it surely can be attempted any time of the year. Pare an apple and, trying not to break the peel, make the longest, continuous piece of apple peel that you can. Throw the peel over your left shoulder. Examine the way the peel has landed and try to figure out what letter it most closely resembles. This letter will be the first letter of your future partner's name. A variation of this is to throw the peel into a cauldron or pot of water.

Another apple divination traditionally performed on Halloween incorporates scrying in a mirror. Sit alone in front of a mirror in a candlelit room. Cut an apple into nine pieces with a knife. Face the mirror while eating the first eight pieces of the apple. Pierce the ninth piece with a knife and hold it over your shoulder. Watch the mirror for a chance to see of vision of your future romantic partner.

Hold an apple by its stem and begin to twist it. As you do this, recite the letters of the alphabet. Whichever letter the stem breaks on will be the first letter of the person you will have a romantic relationship with.

DIVINATION WITH NUTS

Much like with apples, divination with NUTS was an activity traditionally associated with Halloween and Samhain, perhaps in part due to the availability of nuts in autumn. Although different kinds of nuts can be used for divination, it seems hazelnuts are a more popular variety. To ancient Celts and Druids, hazelnuts were associated with inspiration, wisdom, and poetry. Hazel wood was also popular to use for dowsing rods. In Wales, there was a bonfire tradition associated with nuts involving throwing a nut into the flames of a bonfire. If the flames danced when the nut was thrown in, it would be an exciting and fun year. If the flames did not change when the nut was thrown in, it would be a dull and uneventful year.

Here are a few more traditional nut divinations to try at Halloween or any other time of year:

◊ Throw two nuts into a fire, both representing a potential romantic couple. If the two nuts pop and fly away from each other, the romance won't result in much luck for the couple. However, if the two nuts stay close to each other and burn steadily, it's a sign of a good match.

◊ Hold a hazelnut and focus on a "yes" or "no" question. Place the hazelnut on a fire. If the nut pops, the answer to the question is "no." If the nut does not pop, the answer is "yes."

◊ This is a party game that feels like a little twist on the Easter and Ostara tradition of hunting for eggs. Collect empty nutshells for this activity. Write small fortunes on small slips of paper, roll them up, place them into the empty nutshells, then reseal the nutshells. Hide the nutshells around the house for party attendees to hunt and collect. They can crack open the nutshells and read their fortunes.

COLCANNON

COLCANNON is a traditional Irish dish that is used for fortune-telling games, often at Halloween. It is a dish made of mashed potatoes, often mixed with onion, kale, cabbage, and parsnips. Small trinkets are mixed into the dish, each one representing a different fortune. Since this is an older, traditional divination game, the meanings of each trinket are likewise older and more traditional. The person to get the ring in their portion would be the first to get married. Getting the coin would foretell of wealth and riches. The thimble would indicate bachelorhood or spinsterhood. And getting the small china doll would indicate having a child within the year. If these are a little out of date for your taste, you can add trinkets with more modern meanings. For example, I may consider adding a charm resembling a feather to indicate travel, or perhaps a charm that looks like a star for good luck.

CREATING YOUR OWN
FUN FOOD DIVINATION

If you are so inspired, consider creating your own kitchen divination system. Perhaps you assign a special meaning to the first snack you pick from a handful of trail mix—maybe the M&M signifies a positive answer, the nut prosperity, and the raisin a negative answer. Maybe water boiling over and spilling onto the stove top signifies an omen of some kind (or maybe it just indicates that you need to watch the stove a little more closely). Maybe you want to divine an omelet, combining the forces of oomancy and tiromancy to see what shapes you get as everything cooks in the pan. *The GLAM Witch* author Michael Herkes even created a method of divination using candy hearts for Valentine's Day! However you choose to divine in the kitchen, seek out methods that are not only fun, but meaningful, ways to receive omens and tell fortunes.

CHAPTER TWELVE

FOREST DIVINATION

T HE FOREST HAS ALWAYS BEEN CONSIDERED A PLACE where the wild and mysterious thrive, a place where the supernatural and magical can easily manifest away from the civilized eye of town life. There are many forms of divination that can be practiced in the forest and, as you will discover in this section, many forms which require your own intuition and personal interpretations.

ORNITHOMANCY

Divination of observing birds is known as **ORNITHOMANCY**, or **AUGURY**. The types of birds observed, their cries, and the direction in which they fly have been used as means of divining. To begin with ornithomancy, find an area where you would like to observe birds. You may find that in your town there are places or observatories that bird enthusiasts like to visit. Or you may just wish to find a private place in nature and see which birds come visit you first. Does it seem to approach you, or does it observe you from a high branch? If you have a question in mind, it is believed that if a bird appears to your right, the answer is positive. And if the bird appears to your left, the answer is negative. What type of bird is it? You may want to become acquainted with common birds in your area with a bird guide.

For additional information on the spiritual interpretations of birds, I recommend *Birds: A Spiritual Field Guide*, by Arin Murphy-Hiscock. Crows tend to be harbingers of change and psychic abilities, and their closely related counterpart raven teaches of otherworldly connections and witchcraft. Hawks remind us to connect with divinity, enjoy nature, and focus on our health. My mother's favorite, the hummingbird, reminds us to be playful and mindful of time and energy. Owls ask to be keenly observant of life around us, to dig into our knowledge, and to discover our own personal brand of wisdom through meditation and dreamwork. Some say the Fae and forest spirits will leave a feather in your path as a gift and message. With this in mind, consider what type of feather it is and interpret it accordingly.

ANIMAL MESSAGES

When we go into the woods, it is common to have encounters with WILDLIFE. But have you ever gone into the woods and had any unusual interactions with animals? Do you see the same kind of animal repeatedly over a certain period of time? When I was about twenty-five years old I was trying to decide whether to move to England. I asked the universe to show me a sign. After asking for a sign, I received a truly clear animal message while sitting on my parents' back deck in a rural part of Connecticut. I heard a flock of crows flying from the right of me—they were flying low and were incredibly loud. As they flew by, I noticed a fox dash through the yard. It turns out that foxes are linked to Merlin energy, and seeing the crows fly from the right was optimistic. The following fall, I was registered at the University of Nottingham. Have you had special encounters with animals like this as well? Seeing a coyote offers lessons of enduring love and asks you to contemplate trickster energy. Seeing deer asks you to reconnect with family and friends, as well as to practice forgiveness. Seeing a butterfly asks you to allow transformation into your life and to develop your psychic abilities. Seeing a rabbit asks you to focus on your health and on enjoying life and may suggest practicing herbal magic.

SEER IN NATURE

In Scotland, people with "the sight" were called FRITHIRS. They would fast, then just before sunrise, go to their door barefoot and blindfolded. At the doorpost, they would then remove the blindfold and the first thing they would see was considered a significant sign and interpreted for oracle.

Dr. Bluestone, in *How to Read Signs and Omens in Everyday Life*, offers a more modernized approach to the *frithir* ritual. Go to a quiet place outdoors where you will not be interrupted by noise or bothered by other people. Stand still with your eyes closed, then slowly turn around three times clockwise. Open your eyes and focus on the first object you see. Another similar method for seeing into the forest is as follows: Allow your eyes to go unfocused and slowly look around you. What is the first thing your eyes focus on? Is it something moving? Is it something otherworldly? Do you feel an important message from what you witnessed?

SCRYING IN THE FOREST

Some people will suggest you find a calm body of water and SCRY in the moonlight. Others may even suggest gazing into a babbling brook with the sunlight sparkling on the surface. There is an old belief that Druids would stand behind a waterfall and scry through the falling water. Experiment with whatever is not only most comfortable for you but what is safest. Take time to stare into the surface of the water, letting your vision go fuzzy. When thoughts or outside distractions creep into your mind, let them wash away in the water. What do you see? How do you feel? Some people say they see things in the scrying surface, while others feel or hear things. If nothing else, enjoy it as a soothing opportunity to meditate and connect with the element of water.

DIVINATION WITH ACORNS

QUERCUSMANCY is divination using acorns or oak trees. A traditional acorn reading would have been used to predict a couple's romantic outcome. Take two acorns and place them in a bowl of water. If they float to the top together, the couple will get married; if the acorns stay close together, the couple will remain close; but if they float away from each other, the romance may not be quite as fortuitous. We can take acorn divination out of coupling omens as well. They can help you make decisions between two options of any variety. Let's take two job options, for example. Assign one option to one acorn, and the other option to another acorn. Place them in a bowl of water. The acorn to float to the top is the better option. Or, if they both float to the top, note which one makes it to the surface first—that is the option you should go with. You can also ask a yes or no question with two acorns. Ask the question and place the acorns in a bowl of water. If the acorns float together the answer is yes, if they float apart the answer is no.

FLOROMANCY

FLOROMANCY is divination using flowers, and through my research, I've seen that many of the divinations using flowers tend to be folkloric in style. For example, there is the old tradition of pulling petals from a daisy and saying, "He loves me, he loves me not," to determine if your love is requited. It is believed that the first wildflower you see in the spring can give an outlook on the coming year. Seeing a daffodil is considered unlucky. Seeing a rose suggests coming love. Having hiked in my Appalachian neck of the woods at springtime, I can extend this list with my own offerings for first spring flowers. Seeing bloodroot first shows that your year will be one that develops courage and passion, as you will focus on what you love most. Seeing dandelions first means you must focus your intent on manifesting wishes into reality. If the first flower you see is trillium, your year will be focused on the divine feminine, goddess teachings, and good luck. If the first flower you see is jack-in-the-pulpit, your year will be focused on the masculine divine, Green Man energy, and primal desires.

In Sasha Fenton's *Fortune Teller's Handbook*, the author discusses a unique floromancy technique that involves examining flowers picked from a vase. Here I have modified this technique to use in the woods. Find a patch of common wildflowers, such as violets or red clovers. Close your eyes and move your hands over the flowers with the intention of picking a flower that represents how you are in the present moment. When you have found a flower that feels right for your reading, pick it and examine it. The stem of the flower represents the present moment. If it is strong and smooth, this indicates that things are going well in the present; whereas, if it is weak or worn, it could indicate difficult patches. The higher you go up the stem, the more likely you are to see what is to come. New stem growth could indicate new opportunities or events that change the current path you are on. The flower represents the future. A bud represents new opportunities and options. A wide-open flower indicates abundance and fulfillment. If there are sickly petals, this could indicate challenges, while insect bites could indicate things that are out of your control.

Another form of floromancy comes from Victorian tradition. Take two flowers that have not yet blossomed and assign them to two people in a relationship. If the two flowers intertwine, the couple will get married. Flowers that blossom indicate children; however, if the flowers wilt and die, so will the relationship.

CASTING OF FOREST LOTS

It is important to remember that if you are in public woods, it is often prohibited to remove or disturb any of the plant or wildlife. If you are on private land and have permission to do so, collect small items, such as empty snail shells, dried juniper berries, acorns, special stones, pinecones, seeds, leaves, and so on. Give an interpretation to each item and cast them like you would with other sets of divination. For example, acorns are symbols of wisdom and are sacred to the Druids. Pinecones can be symbols of protection and purification. Create interpretations based on what is best for you from your own research and intuition. If you are familiar with runes, you may want to take a walk in nature and see which runes you naturally come across. Sometimes sticks will naturally be laid out in a path in the position of a perfect runic message.

CHAPTER THIRTEEN

GRAPHOLOGY

G RAPHOLOGY IS THE ART OF ANALYZING HANDWRITING TO gain insight into the writer's personality, mood, feelings, or life skills. Although not necessarily a way to see into future events, graphology can be a useful—perhaps even entertaining—tool or exercise to try with friends or divination clients. Graphology looks at the shape, pressure, and style of handwriting. The location of letters, words, and their shapes are also examined to create interpretations about the person writing. Even the way a writer fills out a page or an envelope can be examined for insight. Graphology can be an incredibly in-depth and complex study. The following will give you some basic ways to examine what your handwriting says about you:

The quick brown fox...

SIZE OF LETTERS

◊ If you write large letters, you are an outgoing person and more extroverted. You want people to understand and notice you.

◊ If you write small letters, you are a focused person and more introverted. You want to understand concepts and have good concentration.

Letter Location

◊ You may be reading a lie if the letters are inconsistent in shape and size.

◊ If words are written in a straight line, it can indicate emotional stability, calmness, and composure.

◊ If the words are rigid, there is a fear of losing control.

◊ If the words move up and down or appear all over the place, there may be feelings of indecision.

◊ If the words rise upward across the page, there may be feelings of ambition or optimism.

Pressure of Writing

◊ If you write with heavy pressure, you may be emotional and intense. Heavy pressure can also show stress or anger.

◊ If you write with light pressure, you may be flexible and easygoing. Light pressure can also show sensitivity, low energy, and gentleness.

Slant of Letters

◊ If your words slant to the right, you are social, friendly, and impulsive. Friends and family mean the most to you, and you also like to meet new people.

◊ If your words slant to the left, you are introspective, reserved, and quiet.

◊ If your words do not slant, you are pragmatic and logical but also adaptable.

Space Between Letters

◊ If you have large spaces between letters, you are independent and freethinking.

◊ If you have smaller spaces between letters, you like the company of others and tend to keep a busy schedule.

Loops in "L"s

◊ If you loop your "L"s, you are hopeful and dreamy.
◊ If you retrace your "L"s (no loop), you are tenser or less hopeful about the future.

Loops and Crosses in "T"s

◊ If you loop your "T"s, you are sensitive and do not take criticism well.
◊ If you retrace your "T"s (no loop), you are a hard worker.
◊ If you cross your "T"s high, you are optimistic and ambitious.
◊ If you cross your "T"s in the middle, you are confident.
◊ If you cross your "T"s low, you struggle with self-esteem or making large goals for yourself.

Dots Over "I"s

◊ If you make circular dots over your "I"s, you are artistic and playful.
◊ If you have a simple dot over your "I"s, you are detail-oriented.
◊ If the dot is high over the "I," you have a vivid imagination.
◊ If the dot is to the left of the "I," you are a procrastinator.
◊ If the dot is to the right of the "I," you are organized and detail-oriented.

CHAPTER FOURTEEN

GROUP DIVINATION

I F YOU ARE LOOKING FOR A BONDING ACTIVITY with a spiritual group of friends or a coven with whom you practice magic and witchcraft, look no further than group divination. Working divination with a group allows you to practice divination in a safe setting and gain insight from a variety of people while having a lot of fun.

DIVINATION IN ROUNDS

Instead of speed dating, why not try SPEED READING? This is a great way to practice divination and get many varied readings in the process. For this group activity, ask everyone to bring their favorite divination tool—tarot cards, oracle cards, runes, etc. Have everyone pair off and set a timer for five minutes. One person from each pair starts with a reading, then after five minutes the second person in the pair does a reading. After the second person has finished their reading, have each of the pairs separate and pair up with someone new, kind of like musical chairs.

DIVINATION STATIONS

This activity is a variation on "DIVINATION IN ROUNDS." Set up different spots in a room—or any number of rooms—with a different type of divination in each spot. I call each of these spots "Divination Stations." At one station you can have tarot cards, at another oracle cards, at another palmistry, at another pendulums, and so on. Have as many or as few as you would like. Split your group or coven into equal parties of three to five people. Have them start at one station, allowing them to work with the divination tools at each station for twenty minutes. When the time is up, each group rotates to another station until they have all tried each of the divination methods.

STUDYING A NEW FORM
OF DIVINATION TOGETHER

STUDY a new form of divination with a close group of friends. This could be an especially magical endeavor with a spiritual group or coven. Each time you meet, have a new divination system to focus on or take several meetings to master a single form of divination. If there is anyone in the group who is already mastered in that form of divination, allow them to take the lead in the discussion.

PSYCHOMETRY

An interesting way to do divination in a group is with PSYCHOMETRY, which is the divination of reading an object. This object is usually a special trinket: a piece of jewelry, an amulet (special magically charged object for good luck), or a photograph. The object could also be a piece of furniture, a magical tool, or anything special to its owner. To try psychometry, hold the object and try to get a psychic impression from it. If you are trying psychometry on a larger object like a house or stone, you can simply place your hands on the object. You may feel a certain way holding it, perhaps receiving a clairvoyant vision or clairaudient message. Try to pick up on your initial reactions and allow your first intuitive hits to help you determine the values, feelings, and events that take place with the object you are holding.

For this group activity, ask each person to bring a special object to practice with. I recommend smaller, lighter objects, such as favorite pieces of jewelry. However, I've seen this done with crystals, keys, and foreign coins too. It's preferable to use an object that has been carried or used frequently. Seal the envelope or conceal it in a small bag so people cannot see what it is and allow each person to hold it. After everyone has shared their insight, open the envelope or bag to reveal what the object is. This is also a fun way to share stories or even learn more about the owner of the object.

STREAM OF CONSCIOUSNESS/ AUTOMATIC WRITING EXERCISE

As discussed in Chapter Five (page 51), AUTOMATIC WRITING is a form of divination that, as the name implies, uses writing as a means to acquire messages. The unusual thing about automatic writing is that the writer is supposed to allow the writing utensil to move of its own accord. One exercise that goes along with automatic writing is called "stream of consciousness" writing. This is when you just write, not looking at what is being written, intuitively writing the first things that come to your mind.

To try this exercise with a group, get a blank piece of lined paper. Begin the top of the page with a question or theme you would like people to write about. Pass the page to the person on your right, letting them respond to the passage above. When they are done writing, have them fold over the first entry, so only the prior line shows. Follow this pattern around the table, making sure to fold the paper over so only the previous response is showing for the next writer. When the paper returns to the original owner, he or she can share the entire message with the group.

FORTUNE FOODS

There are many divination games that can be played with FOOD. From colcannon to fortune cookies, there are a number of dishes you can make to entertain your friends with food divination. You can read more about them in Chapter Eleven (page 104). Another fun activity is writing small fortunes inside napkins. Fold the napkins up and place them at each seat, letting the people know that they've received a special fortune at their meal setting.

TAROT PARLOR GAME

This game with tarot cards was used in Renaissance parlors and may be considered one of the first instances in which TAROT was used as a means of divination. Tarot cards, specifically the Major Arcana cards within the tarot deck, were used to describe the personalities of the participants. For this game, a Major Arcana card, like the Hermit or the Empress, would be assigned to a person at a gathering, and the other members of the group would explain why it had been attributed to that individual. Ask each member playing to pick a Major Arcana card, not yet sharing what they pulled with the other members. Through a "Twenty Questions" kind of setup, each person goes around to ask a question about an attribute of the potential card picked. The person holding the card can only answer "yes" or "no." The first person to guess the right card wins the round.

A fun alternative to enjoy tarot in a playful way is for each member to pull a card but refrain from looking at it. The member holds the card up so the other people playing can see it. The member can then ask questions to the other members for divination answers and insights. After asking a few questions, the person holding up the card can try to guess which it is.

ACTING OUT TAROT CARDS

Please note that this can be done with any form of divination, though I have only tried it with TAROT and think it is something aspiring thespians would really enjoy. You can start with one person pulling a card. Have that person talk about the card they pulled and what is happening in that card. Then have the person speak about the card as if they are the card. For example, if I pulled The Fool, I may say something like, "I am feeling really high energy right now, like I could do anything I wanted to!"

Next, another person can pull another card and speak about it. For example, this person pulls the Five of Pentacles and says, "I'm a little concerned that I don't have everything I need to be safe and secure." Now, have the two people, playing the roles of the cards they picked, interact with each other. In this example, perhaps the Five of Pentacles would say to The Fool, "Do you have everything you need for a safe adventure?" Or maybe The Fool would say to the Five of Pentacles, "I don't think you see the freedoms and opportunities that you have." These are just examples, but you get the picture. You can have as many people participate in this exercise as you'd like. I love it because it really helps people get a holistic view of the cards, allowing them to see how their interpretations are shaped simply by being in the presence of other cards.

CHAPTER FIFTEEN

HYDROMANCY:

Water Divination

O NE ANCIENT METHOD OF HYDROMANCY REQUIRES A RING on a string and a jar with water. If you want to try this, lower the ring or other type of pendulum into the water and shake the jar. The number of times the ring or pendulum hits the sides of the jar can help predict the future. One way to consider interpreting this is if it hits the jar an even number of times, the answer is "yes." If it hits the jar an odd number of times, the answer is "no." If it doesn't hit the sides of the jar, then ask again later. If it hits the sides only a few times, or slowly, the outcome will be slow to reveal itself. If it hits the sides frequently or quickly, the outcome will be more immediate.

Another ancient method of hydromancy involves throwing pebbles into water and studying the ripples and sounds the water makes after the object is in the water. If you want to try this, throw a pebble into a body of water and watch the ripples it makes. Do they expand far out? Perhaps the farther out the ripples expand, the more optimistic the reading is. Do you see a certain number of rings? This may be an indication of time or amount. You may also want to try throwing herbs on top of water, and much like reading tea leaves, read the shapes the herbs take on the water's surface.

LECANOMANCY

Lecanomancy is the divination of oil on water. Prophets in Babylon would mix water and oil to foretell the future. Ancient Egyptians also employed this form of divination by filling a bronze bowl with water and covering it with a film of oil to divine from. If you are interested in trying this, take a bowl of warm water and pour a small amount (maybe a teaspoon) of oil onto the water.

Read the shapes that the oil makes in the water, and consider the following interpretations:

◊ If there is an unbroken ring of oil, the answer is positive.
◊ If the oil covers the entire surface, the answer is negative.
◊ Small droplets of oil can signify money.
◊ If there are two divided sections of oil, there may be turmoil or drama ahead.
◊ Crescents or star shapes in the oil are fortunate omens of good luck.

CHAPTER SIXTEEN

MEDIUMSHIP
AND THE SEANCE

MEDIUMSHIP IS THE PSYCHIC ABILITY TO BE ABLE to communicate with the spirits of those who have passed over. Those who practice mediumship speak to spirits through clair-abilities, as mentioned in the first chapter. Mediumship is a topic that requires its own book, though I think it is worth at least mentioning here, since it is something that many people are interested in. I cannot give advice on how to become a medium, but as someone who has always been sensitive to and aware of spirits, I can share with you my personal experiences. Perhaps this can also give you the opportunity to determine whether mediumship or a séance is something that you would like to be involved in.

WHAT IS A SÉANCE?

A SÉANCE is a gathering of people who come together to try and communicate with the spirits of the dead. When we think of séances, we commonly envision old black-and-white photos of spiritualists sitting around a table holding hands. Unfortunately, many spiritualist mediums were inauthentic, leading to skepticism about the validity of séances. However, people have been communicating with the dead for most of history. From Ancient Greek oracles to Ouija boards, the Witch of Endor to *Ghost Hunters*, people have attempted to reach out and speak with the spirits of the dead through the ages. A séance is just a space committed to spirit communication where those present can hope to interact with spirits.

MY EXPERIENCE WITH
SÉANCES AND MEDIUMSHIP

It has been a long time since I have led a SÉANCE. I used to do them more frequently years ago. I worked at a shop in Connecticut where I hosted séances for the public, working as a medium to reach out to spirits who wished to speak with their families and friends. People would come sit in a circle of chairs or at a table around me and listen to any messages I had to share. In many cases, it was an interactive experience where the people present at the séance could ask questions of the spirits through me. In these experiences, I would begin a session by meditating and using my mind's eye to see and hear spirits. Oftentimes, it was through one of my spirit guides that I was able to reach out to certain spirits. I had no formal training, just an interest in seeing if I could work with spirits and see them in my mind as vividly as I felt their presence.

When I moved to Nashville, I reconnected with the world of mediumship by joining a paranormal research team. I worked as the medium with this team to communicate with spirits at various haunted locations. Again, I would go into a meditative state and, through clairvoyance and clairaudience, was able to pass along messages from visiting spirits. Mediumship has since faded out of my life, as my focus has centered on tarot reading and writing. A few years ago, I hosted a séance for the first time in a while and collected the following notes and rules to consider, for those interested in hosting their own séance.

Rule 1: Do Research on Mediumship and Séances.

Before leaping into a séance, take time to do research and study the history and practice of spirit communication. Read about mediumship and do research on what it entails. Two books worth reading during your exploration of spirit communication include *Buckland's Book of Spirit Communication* and *Magickal Mediumship* by Danielle Dionne. A séance is not something to do for kicks and giggles, on a whim, or without experience and safety measures. If you have never done mediumship work before, please speak with someone who has and get guided assistance through a séance. If you are not comfortable with Ouija boards or spirit boards, then don't use them, though we will cover that later in this chapter. I think the best way to learn how to go about performing a séance is to speak to mediums, have conversations with people who have been in or led séances, and study whatever you can find on spirit communication.

Rule 2: Find the Right Space for your Séance.

You will want to create a dark, quiet, safe, comfortable space for a séance. I personally believe the space should be clear of clutter and feel welcoming. This can also mean that you want to find a space that is respectful to those around you. In other words, if you have a roommate who doesn't want anything to do with a séance, don't conduct one at the kitchen table in your shared space.

Rule 3: Prepare a Safe Space Prior to the Séance.

To further create a safe place for a séance, consider doing some or all of the following:

◊ Start by cleansing everyone with rosemary or another cleansing herb.

Continue by cleansing the area where the séance would be conducted. I also liked to keep a small cauldron in the center of the séance area with frankincense and myrrh incense in it.

◊ Offer spring water mixed with sea salt to those present who wish to further cleanse and purify themselves and the space.

◊ Share a protection oil with everyone in attendance, and allow them to anoint themselves. A simple protection oil can be equal parts frankincense, rosemary, and juniper essential oils. I would also anoint black candles with the protection oil and place them on the séance table.

◊ Prior to the séance, have everyone take three deep breaths together, in and out. Ask them to visualize white light energy surrounding them and the séance circle.

◊ Say a prayer or open with an incantation asking that only higher, well-intentioned spirits come forward to speak.

Rule 4: Have Manageable Activities During the Séance.

The most recent séance I hosted lasted about an hour. If you do not have mediumship experience, there are other activities you can try to see if spirits make themselves known. Place a glass of water on the table and ask the spirit if they can touch the water. Watch to see if there are any ripples in the water. You can also ask a spirit to make itself known by flickering candles or making sounds. Some people will ask them to make a knocking sound. You can also use a pendulum to ask "yes" or "no" questions, allowing participants to ask questions. You may also wish to use your favorite divination kit during the session, asking the spirit questions and drawing from your divination kit to assist with receiving an answer.

At the more recent séance I hosted, I asked if the spirits could make sounds to let us know if they were there—I asked the spirits to knock on the wall or make a sound. I knocked on the table, asking them to repeat it back. Sadly, no knocks were heard. Without much physical interaction we decided to try contacting spirits through spiritual methods. I did a small meditation to quiet myself and try to connect with spirits through mediumship. Oftentimes, when I am doing mediumship, I see spirits with my mind's eye. That time, very little came through on its own. I asked the séance participants if they had anyone they'd like to speak to. One of my own spirit guides came through—a young girl named Kayla, who specifically asked for candy to be put on the table. As per her request, sweets were added to the table. We continued by asking questions; we asked whether she could help bring forward other spirits, but, alas, that did not happen. We then tried using a pendulum, which was a more successful tactic for that particular séance.

One interesting element that you may enjoy using in your séance is a small, handheld voice recorder. If you and those in attendance are comfortable with the session being recorded, a voice recorder may capture electronic voice phenomenon, or EVPs, audio that may not be audible to the untrained ear but may be captured in the recording and heard when played back. It is believed that EVPs are paranormal in natural, possibly being messages from spirits. However you decide to manage your time during the session, be sure to maintain thoughtful, quiet pauses to allow the spirits to respond.

RULE 5: CLOSE THE SÉANCE WITH GROUNDING AND CLEANSING.
As with the opening of the séance you will want to close with grounding and cleansing activities. Here are some to consider:

◊ Have a closing incantation where you thank the spirits for coming forward and sharing a space with them. Tell them the séance has ended and say goodbye to them. Clap three times or ring a bell to close the session.

◊ Allow the participants to stand and stretch. This can be a good grounding point where everyone can yawn, move around, and touch the ground.

◊ Cleanse the area where the séance was held again, as well as the participants if they so wish.

◊ Allow participants to cleanse themselves with Florida Water, a mixture of water and various oils that is said to be energetically cleansing and purifying. You can splash the water on your hands or chakra points.

REFLECTIONS ON HOSTING A SÉANCE

No matter how people feel about séances, the desire to contact the dead will never go out of style. If you are ready and willing, a séance is a fascinating activity to try. It's important to keep in mind that connecting with the dead is not a scientific routine: you can't make assumptions as to what will happen in a séance. A séance is not a simple, light-hearted activity, nor is it an activity for anyone to try out of sheer curiosity. It takes energetic effort, spiritual research, and respect for spirits and the spirit world. If you are not sure you want to host a séance, consider sitting in on a paranormal investigation instead. Paranormal investigators have all sorts of cool electronic equipment to communicate with, such as EMF detectors or ghost boxes, which are said to speak the words a spirit is trying to share with the living. Sometimes these pieces of equipment catch paranormal activity more than a séance itself might.

TO OUIJA...

Slumber parties weren't complete without spooky games. Bloody Mary, Light as a Feather (Stiff as a Board), and the Sandman game, to name a few, gave the late night a scary, yet exciting edge. Young attendees could giggle and scream when trying to conjure spirits or levitate, passing the time into the wee hours of the morning while exploring the supernatural in a seemingly innocent way. However, there is one slumber party fixture guaranteed to add a spooky and exciting edge that beats the others: the Ouija board.

Spirit boards are a way of communication with spirits by spelling out words with a board. The spirit board has letters of the alphabet written on it—additionally, the numbers 0 through 9 and the words "yes" and "no" are applied. Some boards also feature "hello" and "goodbye." There is a small tool called a planchette that moves over the spirit board, which is said to be controlled and moved by the spirit wishing to come forward and speak. Participants in a spirit board session will each place a hand on the planchette, though they are not supposed to manipulate its motion. Participants can ask questions of spirits present, and if any are indeed amongst them, they can come forward and answer questions through the board.

The most famous of spirit boards is the Ouija, which has been the topic of speculation and scary stories since its creation. The Ouija was invented by Elijah Bond and Washington Bowie, who created Kennard Novelty Company to make and market the boards in 1890. The name of the board itself was conjured through a mediumship session with Helen Peters, Bond's sister-in-law. She claimed to have the word given to her, and when asked about the meaning of "Ouija," the response was "good luck." The board was a success, marketed as both an entertaining toy and a mystifying tool for communication with spirits.

The Ouija was a product of the spiritualist movement, which utilized it to communicate with spirits in an efficient manner. With the Ouija, anyone could be a medium and speak to those from the great beyond. It has been argued to be a hoax, and on the other end, it has a reputation of being a tool of the devil. But how could a game harbor such dreadful intentions?

The use of the Ouija board has been reported to welcome the presence of ghostly and demonic spirits. Paranormal investigators have also observed that many places with haunted activity stem from the use of the Ouija board. On the other hand, scientists say that the Ouija's planchette is moved by automatic muscle movements that we do not intentionally recognize. As a result, many people believe that the Ouija board is either an ineffective game or a portal to negativity. Another perspective is that spirit boards can be an effective means of divination with research, practice, and protection.

...OR NOT TO OUIJA?

Witch Way Magazine's Tonya A. Brown and I had a great conversation about the Ouija board and whether it is safe. I am of the mindset that it is not the safest instrument to use, whereas Tonya believes that it is a divination tool like any other if used with the right frame of mind. Both of us have great opinions about this, shaped by our own experiences and the stories of others.

Tonya believes that the Ouija board starts off as a neutral divination tool and that it is up to the practitioner to become familiar with it. She points out that the Ouija has been around for a very long time: if it opened a portal to demons and evil every time it was used, we'd be living in a real-life Hellmouth! She argues, "Using a Ouija board is like dialing a random number and chatting with whoever is on the other side, just like a pendulum. All forms of divination are created equally."

Having seen the effects of a Ouija board through paranormal research, my personal belief is that it is unsafe when used by inexperienced people who do not take it seriously. The Ouija board is accessible to a population that is young and inexperienced with mediumship. Without caution, without practice, anyone can put their hands on the planchette to speak with uncommon forces. The Ouija board (nowadays) is made with cardboard, conveniently folded and packaged for mass-production. Instead of being a unique, well-crafted tool, it is labeled an entertaining game and sold in toy stores.

Arguably, many divinatory tools are mass produced, so what's the difference between a Ouija board and a tarot deck manufactured by the company US Games? It is the audience who uses the tools. Someone who purchases a tarot deck or a pendulum has considered the tool's psychic abilities. They also recognize that using the divination tool will take a considerable amount of time to practice and perfect. When the Ouija board or tarot deck is available in the board game section of a toy store, it's not going to be taken seriously; therefore, the results are not going to be serious. What if spirit boards were approached differently? Could Tonya's opinion sway me if proper precautions were taken to treating a spirit board as a sacred divination tool?

SAFETY PRECAUTIONS FOR OUIJA BOARDS

Ultimately, consider using the Ouija with great caution. If you use it, read up on its history and gather opinions about how people feel about using it. Do your research! Consider that there are spirit boards on the market other than a Ouija board. Perhaps something handmade with protective symbols is more along the lines of what you are interested in working with. Before thinking of doing any work with spirit boards, consider whether it is truly necessary to use a spirit board at all. Before your session, ask yourself what it is you want to use a spirit board for. Who do you want to contact? Why do you want to contact them? Is it a healthy pursuit? Be mindful of how you feel during the session. What kinds of messages are you receiving? Do you feel comfortable or uncomfortable?

There are magical ways of creative a protective space. A circle of salt can create a protective border around the area where the board is being used. Crystals like jet, obsidian, and hematite can be used for grounding, protection, and absorbing negativity. Cleansing an area with herbs before and after a session can clear out any negative or stagnant energy as well. If you are unsure of what you are dealing with supernaturally, have less training in the psychic arts, or don't know how to protect yourself from energetic harm, you may want to just steer clear. There are plenty of other ways to celebrate a night with friends: Midnight Margaritas and a *Charmed* marathon are the first ideas that come to my mind!

CHAPTER SEVENTEEN

NUMEROLOGY

N UMEROLOGY IS THE STUDY AND ANALYSIS OF NUMBERS. This form of divination assigns numbers spiritual lessons, personality traits, and mystical messages. The practice of numerology dates back to the Greek mathematician Pythagoras, who was said to have acquired his knowledge of numbers in Egypt. Single-digit numbers are assigned specific meanings and can indicate personality traits, potential future events, and spiritual insight. These single-digit numbers are broken down from birthdays, names, and words. There are two numbers that are not reduced to a single digit: 11 and 22, which are said to be "master numbers."

Multi-digit numbers (anything 10 and above) can be broken down into single-digit numbers to determine numerological significance by adding the numerals together. For example, the number 31 can be broken down by adding 3 and 1 to get 4; 1991 can be broken down by adding 1, 9, 9, and 1 to get 20, which is reduced to 2 (since 2 and zero added together equals 2).

Please note that different sources on numerology have various methods of discovering calculations and labeling numbers. I have followed the work of Joy Woodward in *A Beginner's Guide to Numerology* because it is an excellent source with easy-to-follow constructive information. Below you will find that there are different numerological calculations, followed by a master list of what each of the numbers mean. You will find that many numbers can help to support the magic, purpose, and lessons in your life.

BIRTHDAY NUMBER

The BIRTHDAY NUMBER is represented by the day you were born and can reveal special talents and lessons you will face during your lifetime. I'm going to share my challenging birthday and life path numbers with you, as I was astonished by how much the lessons and opportunities these numbers revealed resonated with me. I was born on June 19, 1981. My birthday number is 19, a karmic debt number (see below for more information) that can be reduced to the number 1.

LIFE PATH NUMBER

Your LIFE PATH NUMBER is the month, day, and year you were born. The life path number is said to represent the lessons you must face during your life.

It would be calculated as follows, again using my birthday as the example:

June 19th, 1981

June is the 6th month, so June equals the number 6

The 19th day calculates to... (1+9=10) then take the 10 and add the 1 and 0 together (1+0=1)

The year 1981 calculates to... (1+9+8+1=19) then take the 19 and add the 1 and 9 together (1+9=10) then take the 10 and add 1 and 0 together (1+0=1)

Then, take the sums of each equation, the red numbers, and add them together for your Life Path Number... (6+1+1=8)

DESTINY NUMBER

Numerology also converts letters into numbers. The numbers uncovered from names can reveal personality traits. By using the chart below, you can convert letters into numbers. Your DESTINY NUMBER is calculated by converting the letters of your full name (as it appears on your gift certificate) then adding the numbers together until they are reduced to a single-digit number.

1	2	3	4	5	6	7	8	9
A	B	C	D	E	F	G	H	I
J	K	L	M	N	O	P	Q	R
S	T	U	V	W	X	Y	Z	

PERSONALITY NUMBER

Your PERSONALITY NUMBER shows how you reveal yourself to the world, your outer motives. I equate this to the astrological sun signs. This number is calculated using the consonants in your name.

SOUL NUMBER

Your SOUL NUMBER shows your inner workings and heart's desires. This is your inner world. I equate it to the astrological moon signs. This number is calculated using the vowels in your name.

OTHER NUMEROLOGICAL INDICATORS

◊ Combine and compare your birthday and life path numbers.

◊ Your first initial can show the qualities you want others to notice about you first.

◊ The first vowel in your name can show how you react instinctively to situations.

◊ Compare your given name's numerology to your nickname's numerology to see where you are making personal transformations.

◊ Consider calculating your birth month and day with the current year to see significant lessons and opportunities for the current year.

◊ Look for repeating numbers appearing in your life. These repeating numbers can show themselves in a variety of ways: notable times (11:11 is a common one), numbers on receipts, or even numbers you hear. Some believe these are nods from spirit guides, sending you affirmations and messages.

◊ Consider using the letter-to-number chart to decipher the numerological meaning of powerful words of importance to you. This could be the name of a place, a word you keep hearing over and over again, or even a favorite song verse or incantation.

KARMIC DEBT NUMBERS

There are specific numbers that can appear in numerology that represent KARMIC DEBTS, which are said to be lessons you need to learn in this life from unfavorable behavior or situations from past lives. These challenging numbers can indicate that you perhaps didn't use your powers and abilities in past lives with the best of intentions. Karmic debt numbers can bring challenging (and sometimes repetitive) lessons into your current life until debts are resolved through healthy pursuits. I found this fascinating, since I carry a doozy of a karmic debt number, simply based on my day of birth—19—but also have 16 in my birthday number. These are not pleasurable or easy numbers to carry but instead represent challenges and opportunities for growth. My hope is that in sharing this with you, if you do encounter these numbers, you resonate with their lessons and can find ways to clear the debt and not have to live through the issues again and again.

† 13 indicates the misuse of time or not using time productively. This could indicate that in a past life you were lazy. In this life, you can pay this debt by working extra hard, contemplating how control factors into your life, and fighting the urge to procrastinate. I think of the Death card in tarot with this one. What can you do to allow for momentum in your life so you can celebrate transformation and evolution?

† **14** indicates the misuse of earthly pleasures and forming addictions. This could indicate that in a past life you overindulged in decadences and focused solely on physical gratification. In this life, you can pay this debt by resisting temptation, understanding why you desire escape, and helping others with addiction issues. I think of the tarot card Temperance with this one. Where has moderation helped you find balance and healing in your life?

† **16** indicates the misuse of love and creating toxic relationships. This could indicate that in a past life you were not kind-hearted or honest in matters of love. In this life, you can pay this debt by working through relationship issues in an open and vulnerable manner, making heartfelt choices based on the loving development of a relationship. I think of The Tower tarot card with this one. What actions can you take to avoid being in spaces of destruction and chaos?

† **19** indicates the misuse of power and calculated steps to generate fear for personal gain. This could indicate that in a past life you abused a position of leadership, even one connected to spirituality and knowledge. In this life, you can pay this debt by supporting those who have less for themselves and by lessening harsh criticisms of others. I think of The Sun tarot card with this one. What can you do to illuminate joy and generate growth for those around you?

NUMEROLOGY INTERPRETATIONS

† **NUMBER 1:** One represents independence, new beginnings, self-development, individuality, creativity, and incentive. Ones have strong-willed personalities, make excellent leaders, and have bright, courageous original ideas. They can be selfish and stubborn and should learn to work better with others. Those who have one in their lives focus on independence and resourcefulness. It's also important to try and stay focused on one project

at a time, ensuring follow through to see its outcome. Ones make excellent managers, lawyers, engineers, writers, directors, and business owners because of their cleverness and resourcefulness. They are compatible with twos, fours, and sevens.

† NUMBER 2: Two represents attraction, diplomacy, balance, empathy, intuition, cooperation, and receptivity. Twos are generous, adaptable, and sensitive peacemakers who work well with others. They can be moody, dishonest, and feel uncomfortable with too many responsibilities. While they focus their lives on their relationships, they must learn about how to stand out on their own and celebrate the blessings of solitary pauses. They make excellent bookkeepers, politicians, musicians, artists, and hospitality workers. They are compatible with ones and sevens.

† NUMBER 3: Three represents self-expression, expansion, openness, imagination, ambition, creativity, art, and cycles. Threes are creative people who are also social, fun, and outgoing. They can be jealous and hypocritical. Those who have three in their lives focus on creative expression but need to learn how to share the spotlight with others. They make excellent entertainers, actors, social workers, and administrators. They are compatible with sixes and nines.

† NUMBER 4: Four represents foundations, organization, productivity, practicality, order, truth, and stability. Fours are serious people who like to work hard and see tangible results. They can be stubborn, narrow-minded, and uncomfortable with change. Fours are learning how to release controlling behaviors. While they love structure and security, there is also a lot to learn in decisions and events that do not fit the mold. Those who have four in their lives focus on how they can help others. They make excellent scientists, military workers, mechanics, and builders. They are compatible with twos and eights.

† **Number 5:** Five represents energy, travel, curiosity, courage, excitement, change, activity, and focus on the physical. Fives are bright people who do well with change and love adventure and memorable moments that make for fascinating stories. They can be easily distracted or thoughtless, and in this life they are learning how stick to commitments and develop rational life choices. Those who have five in their lives focus on learning from experience. They make excellent salespeople and would do well in work dealing with travel. They are compatible with other fives.

† **Number 6:** Six represents harmony, compassion, service, beauty, generosity, service to others, and teaching. Sixes are compassionate people who love to be surrounded by love and beauty. While they can be loving and loyal, they run the risk of becoming selfish, irresponsible, and impractical. Those who have six in their lives focus on following nurturing ideals and healing others. They make excellent healers, cooks, designers, and decorators. They are compatible with threes and nines.

† **Number 7:** Seven represents wisdom, mysticism, birth and rebirth, contemplation, poetry, study, and the esoteric. Sevens are introverted and can be analytical but also sensitive. They can be cynical, withdrawn, or self-absorbed and must learn how to relate to others through active listening. Those who have seven in their lives focus on the spiritual, esoteric, and worldly observation. They make excellent researchers, detectives, musicians, poets, or spiritual leaders. They are compatible with ones, twos, and fours.

† **Number 8:** Eight represents ambition, abundance, self-power, authority, leadership, eccentricity, and transformation. Eights have great organizational skills and have the ambition to succeed at tasks at hand. They can be impatient, unreliable, or lack tact and in this life must learn patience and generosity. Those who have eight in their lives focus on trying to balance spirituality and materialism. They make excellent business owners,

publishers, coaches, executives, promoters, and consultants. While eights are often thought of as financial people, they also represent people who are influential and learning to find balance in their lives. They are compatible with twos, fours, elevens, and twenty-twos.

† NUMBER 9: Nine represents humanitarianism, achievement, inspiration, enlightenment, tolerance, completion, and optimism. Nines are courageous leaders and support systems. They can be wise and witty but also impulsive and nervous, having trouble concentrating. In this life, they are learning about forgiveness and release. Those who have nine in their lives must work to help others find their way. They make excellent social workers, teachers, writers, and inventors. They are compatible with threes and sixes.

† NUMBER 11: Eleven represents illumination, mysticism, intuition, invention, empathy, and psychic abilities and is connected to Jesus. Elevens are visionaries and spend their lives seeking spiritual knowledge. They can be selfish, fanatical, and lack direction. In this life, they must learn how to turn dreams into reality. Eleven represents the need to develop spirituality and pay attention to intuition. Those who have eleven in their lives can inspire others to do good. They make excellent psychics, scientists, healers, and lecturers. They are compatible with twos, fours, eights, and twenty-twos.

† NUMBER 22: Twenty-two represents powerful building, expansion, leadership, and improvement and is connected to Buddha. Twenty-twos can indicate movers and shakers. They are people who can accomplish major successes quickly and also help better futures for others. They can be boastful and self-absorbed and, in this life, must learn how to use their powers for good. They make excellent architects, builders, buyers, health workers, and nonprofit organizers. They are compatible with twos, eights, and elevens.

CHAPTER EIGHTEEN

OGHAM

THE OGHAM HAS A LONG, COMPLEX HISTORY, ONE that has been researched and investigated by modern-day Druids, witches, academics, historians, and mythologists. The origin of the OGHAM is unknown, though there are various proposed theories, one such theory being that the ogham was created as a method of writing after exposure to the Latin language, similarly to the Nordic runes.

There are about three hundred seventy stone inscriptions that show the ogham, and it appears they were in use between 300 and 600 CE. None of these are magical in nature and tend to be place markers for locations in Ireland, Scotland, Wales, the Isle of Man, and England. Inscriptions were usually in Old Irish, Old Welsh, and Latin, often on stone or wood. Ogham engravings have also been found on other items like bone and amber. One example is an egg-shaped amber bead from medieval Ireland that was used as an amulet to aid in childbirth. Much of our knowledge about the ogham comes from a book compiled in 1391 called the *Book of Ballymote*, though its contents are a compilation of documents that date back to the ninth century.

According to Sandra Kynes in *Whispers from the Woods*, the ogham could have been a way to pass along valuable information: "Rather than being an alphabet that was written and read like Latin and Greek, the cryptic characters of the ogham were abstract symbols—'keys' to a wealth of information. If you have tried using the ogham, you will have found that the letters are not practical for writing more than simple instructions," (43). Some have even suggested that the simple lines of the ogham alphabet are pictorial representations of a sign language.

THE OGHAM ALPHABET

THE OGHAM ALPHABET originally had twenty characters, with an additional five characters added later. Each character is commonly assigned a tree association; however, it should be noted that linguists and historians only see the ogham-tree connection dating to late medieval texts. Modern authors have even linked the ogham to months, though there is no historic evidence to suggest this was done by ancient Druids.

The original twenty ogham characters are made up of simple lines, whereas the five added characters were more complex to accommodate Greek and Latin letters. The original twenty characters are called *feda*, and the additional five letters are called *forfeda*. Some people omit using the last five letters of the *forfeda* while doing divination because they were not found on any stone inscriptions and only in very few manuscripts. The characters are divided into groups of five, each called *aicme*. Ogham characters are written down a middle or stem line called a *druim*. When written horizontally, the ogham is read from left to right. When written vertically, the ogham is read from bottom to top.

While there might always be a debate on the ogham's origin and continued reevaluation of their uses, modern-day users and students of the ogham revere the alphabet for its symbolic wisdom. The trees they have come to represent and the Celtic mythology and Druidic history they are a part of make them a valuable tool for witches, Druids, and practitioners of divination. Nigel Pennick, in *Magical Alphabets*, offers the following wisdom for modern explorers of the ogham: "We should not fall into the trap of imagining that the older a system is, then the more 'pure' it must be. . . . Although we study the past, we should remember that it is the repository of errors as well as truths, and enlightened people of the present day can make a contribution to the understanding of divination through alphabets as well as many a practitioner of former times," (127-128).

HOW TO USE OGHAM IN DIVINATION

Historically, there are not many accounts of OGHAM being used in divination; however, the characters have been incorporated into modern studies as a means of examining a situation. Ogham as a form of divination is not simple or straightforward; instead, it offers insight, messages, and wisdom through the knowledge and myths woven into the trees and symbols connected to the various *feda*. The common method of using ogham as divination is to use small sticks with characters carved on them. There are also cards with the ogham on them as well. I have ogham painted onto small discs of birch wood. Some people only use the original twenty *feda*, while others like to incorporate the added five *forfeda* as well.

An easy way to begin working with ogham in divination is to pull one stick or piece from a bag and study its symbolism and significance in divination. You may find that one way you can enhance your understanding of the ogham is to familiarize yourself with the mythology, folklore, magical energies, and healing properties of the trees associated with the ogham. In *Celtic Tree Magic*, Danu Forest suggests pulling three sticks for a reading in a vertical line, like that of a tree trunk. The first stick, in the bottom position, represents the lower world and the roots of your situation. The second stick, in the middle position, represents the middle world and all circumstances that surround the present situation. The third stick, in the top position, represents the upper world, your connection to divinity, and the most benevolent outcome of a situation. Please keep in mind when reviewing the following meanings of the ogham that there are variations on which trees are associated with certain *feda*.

MEANING OF THE OGHAM

AICME BEITH

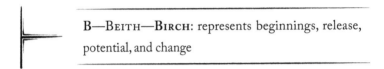

B—Beith—Birch: represents beginnings, release, potential, and change

Beith is generally a sign of good fortune. Birch is sacred to the Mother Goddess and is a tree that shows the first signs of spring. It represents a time to clear away old to make way for new. Mentally prepare for work ahead. It could also indicate an initiation into otherworldly work and signal that it is time to discover wisdom in the initiation and first steps of projects. When birch appears, it is a great time to sweep or do herbal smoke cleansing.

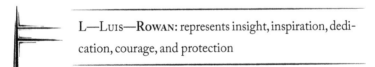

L—Luis—Rowan: represents insight, inspiration, dedication, courage, and protection

Rowan indicates a need to create psychic boundaries around oneself. It appears during a time of overcoming difficulties with imaginative solutions. Stay grounded, use common sense, and practice healing. This is a magical tree associated with faeries and charms.

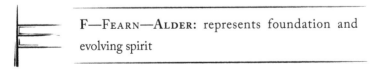

F—Fearn—Alder: represents foundation and evolving spirit

This is an ogham with a warrior spirit and can be supportive, protective, and offer courage if you are facing challenges. Be bold and courageous in your ability to overcome obstacles. Defend yourself in mind, body, and spirit. Know how to shield yourself and create protective boundaries for your own wellness. Consider how music and poetry play a role in your life.

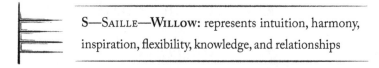

S—Saille—Willow: represents intuition, harmony, inspiration, flexibility, knowledge, and relationships

Since willow resides near moving water, the element of water plays deeply with this *feda*. This can be a time of gently flowing events and moon magic. Pay attention to dreams and messages from the otherworld. Practice forgiveness and compassion and listen to your intuition.

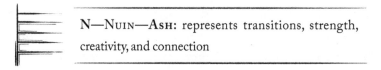

N—Nuin—Ash: represents transitions, strength, creativity, and connection

Now is a time in which focus and determination are needed. Your goal with ash is to stay as active as possible and to hold on to any inspiration you need to keep working. Create mile markers and goal lists to stay focused. Balance work and play. Erynn Rowan Laurie writes in *Ogam: Weaving Word Wisdom* that this *feda*'s magic is for bringing people together for a good cause (76).

AICME HUATH

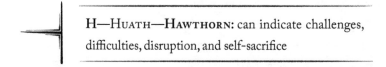

H—Huath—Hawthorn: can indicate challenges, difficulties, disruption, and self-sacrifice

There is a need for strength and hope during this time, as you may be facing a test of some kind. Stay hopeful. These challenges will make you feel stronger and transformed. Rest and heal often during this period to stay well.

D—Duir—Oak: associated with Druids and could indicate shelter or safe spaces

Oak is about strength, confidence, and fate. Answers will be received by going inward at this time. Growth and opportunities of all kinds are available. Practice mindfulness to be in the present moment; this will bring you self-awareness and empowerment.

 T—Tinne—Holly: associated with hearth and home, energy, and courage

There is a need for balance and unity. This may be a time of tests, though these tests will help you develop your spirituality and resilience. Think about things—both metaphorical and real—that light your life in the darkest of times.

 C—Coll—Hazel: represents wisdom, knowledge of secrets, and creativity

It represents the discovery of information and divine inspiration. Now is a time to collect knowledge through research, exploration, and observation.

 Q—Quert—Apple: represents love, faithfulness, happiness, and rebirth

Learn to be kind to yourself and others to feel a sense of wholeness and coming to fruition. Apple could also indicate a spiritual journey. This journey into the unfamiliar could bring discomfort, but generosity, kindness, and faith in yourself will help you reach your destination.

M—Muinn—Blackberry or Vine: indicates inward journeys, learning lessons, and harvest

It is the completion of plans, bounty, and yearning to achieve goals. Contemplate the cycle of planting, growing, and harvesting. Vine can also indicate working closely with others or creating comfort and peace among those you live with.

G—Gort—Ivy: represents growth, development, and confronting the mystical

Changes are necessary for growth and transformation. Seek out a healthy and trustworthy support system. None of us can do everything alone all the time. Ask for help. Pay attention to red flags and warnings. Identify and resolve problems before they get worse.

Ng—Ngetal—Broom or Fern: healing, preservation, gathering, adaptation, and written communication

It shows a need for independence, being resourceful, and thinking outside of the box. Further work is necessary, and it would be best to be flexible right now. If you feel off-balance now is a time to heal and re-center.

St—Straif—Blackthorn: represents authority, control, magical power, initiation, liberation, and rebirth

It can indicate a sudden change and a need to face your fears. If challenges arise now, remember that they will help you mature and bring clarity into your life.

R—Ruis—Elder: represents maturity, self-examination, awareness, and transition

It shows a need for sacrifice and facing your shadow side. It may be a time for you to correct mistakes and missteps. Be mindful not to be too critical and to recognize your achievements. Keep calm and carry on.

AICME AILM

 A—Ailm—Fir or Scots Pine: represents rising above adversity, as well as regeneration and healing

It indicates a time of peace and pause to gain perspective and contemplate next steps. You should not give up—you must follow through with your brilliant ideas. Now may be a time to slow down and remember that slow and steady wins the race.

 O—Onn—Furze or Gorse: Furze represents hope and fertility

You may feel a resurgence of new ideas and inspiration. It is a bright time of pride, empowerment, and fertility. There may be an increase in material possessions.

 U—Ur—Heather: represents passion, generosity, and good luck

Reconnect with loved ones. It is time to trust spirit and the natural flow of the universe. This may be a time to let go of things that no longer serve you, which may help you focus more energy on what is going well for you.

E—Edadh—Aspen or White Poplar: represents communication, success, courage, and animation

Connect with others and get the ball rolling. Though there is spiritual success and prosperity right now, there is a need to remain humble.

I—Idho—Yew: Yew represents transition, changes, and perseverance

Now is the time to reflect on endings and passage. It is a time to practice patience. Think about who and what you love and reflect on all the good that has come through your life.

AICME EABHADH / THE FORFEDA

EA—Eabhadh—Aspen or White Poplar: represents gateways, passages, and assistance in changes

It can indicate being on a path toward wisdom or needing to find this path.

OI—Oir—Spindle Tree: represents creativity, inspiration, and abundant resources

It may be associated with weaving fate and destiny, holding lessons of abundance and prosperity outside of money.

UI—Uinllean—Honeysuckle: represents manifestation, magic, and resistance

Honeysuckle can be healing from grief and releasing emotions that tie you to your past. Learn unconditional love as a means of healing.

IO—IFIN—GOOSEBERRY: represents clarity, psychism, ancestral wisdom, and visions

To see gooseberry is to ask for divinity to be present to offer support and clarity. Divinity is with you and within you when you are ready.

 AE—PHAGOS—WITCH HAZEL: represents cleansing, purification, and crossing over

It could indicate illness and a need to receive healing support of some kind. For me, I have seen witch hazel as representing the need to seek out healing balms for chronic illness, getting to the root cause with health issues, and honoring relief for every moment.

SAMPLE READING

I pulled three *feda* for myself in this ogham reading: the past is represented by heather, the present is represented by spindle, and the future is represented by blackberry or vine. Not surprisingly, these indicate being in a space of creativity in the past and present. It seems fitting while writing a book, as heather indicates a burst of good luck and suggests a time to focus energy. The focus of energy was utilized and came to the spindle tree, which shows a time of creativity and inspiration. This could also indicate that the creative luck hints at art as a viable path for abundance and prosperity. Finally, the reading ends with blackberry or vine, showing the future fruition of a creative project. In a way, this could show the past as being a creative spark, the present as creative work in action, and the future as the rewards of a completed project. If I had to give my future self advice, it would be to reflect on the cycles and timing it took to make the book happen and to have this in mind for future endeavors.

How would you interpret this reading?

CHAPTER NINETEEN

ONEIROMANCY:

Dream Divination

T HINK ABOUT A VIVID DREAM THAT YOU'VE HAD. You may even be able to recall one from childhood. Were you flying in your dream? Did you get to visit a favorite place that you longed to see? Have you had a dream where something came true? Sometimes the memories of dreams can last a lifetime, inspiring us artistically, offering us guidance, or perhaps hinting at events to come. Dreams have long been considered mystical in nature, with some seeing the images and messages in dreams as being divine.

ENHANCING DREAMS

There are natural ways to prepare yourself for an evening of VIVID DREAMS. First, it is important to know that people go through varying cycles of how much they remember from dreams. One night you may not recall anything from dreamland, while the next you feel like you've dreamt an entire movie. If you want to try to have more vivid dreams, consider some of the following tips:

◊ Ensure that you have a consistent sleep cycle. Getting a good night's rest is tough for some, but if you can at least try to get plenty of sleep, this is a great start. Go to bed around the same time every evening and try to wake up at the same time every morning. Sleep in a comfortable, darkened room where you will not be interrupted by noise.

◊ Try a guided visualization meditation before bed. I have found this to be a beneficial way to get in the right state of mind for vivid dreams. Eat melatonin-rich foods. Increased melatonin levels can help you have a deeper, more restful sleep. Melatonin may also enhance the vividness of your dreams. Foods like almonds, cherries, bananas, oatmeal, and sunflower seeds have a healthy amount of melatonin in them and would be a great bedtime snack. Drink tea with mugwort and cinnamon; these herbs can help to enhance the vividness of dreams.

◊ Practice "dream recall." When you wake up in the morning, take a moment to work through your dream. If you feel you can, try to continue the dream in your mind, allowing your mind to revisit, resolve, or conclude the dream.

DREAM MAGIC

After you've eaten all the bananas and cherries you can handle before bedtime, you can enhance the vividness of dreams through MAGICAL means as well. Oils that are beneficial for dreams include jasmine, rose, and sandalwood. A simple oil blend for sweet dreams and restful sleep can be made with one part rose oil, one part jasmine oil, two parts lavender oil, and two parts sandalwood oil. You can also make a dream pillow with herbs to tuck into your pillowcase by using some (or all) of the following: lavender, marjoram, mugwort, calendula, cinquefoil, heliotrope, jasmine, and peppermint. You can also surround your bed with crystals that are said to aid in enhancing vivid dreams. Amethyst, Herkimer diamond, azurite, sodalite, lapis lazuli, ametrine, crystal quartz, and moldavite are some of the crystals commonly used for dreamwork. I have personally had good experiences with vivid dreams when selenite is near my bed.

DREAM JOURNAL

Keeping a JOURNAL by your bedside can be one of the best ways to enhance your dreams. Your dreams will seem more vivid when you take a moment to write about them when you first wake up. You can go back to read about the dream, making it fresh in your mind once again. Keeping a dream journal can be tough, but even if you can scribble down a few important notes from the dream or follow a bullet journal page on dreams, you can keep record of what may be valuable messages. When I was more diligent about keeping a dream journal, I could recall records of addresses, numbers, and names in dreams. Try it for a week, but don't beat yourself up if you miss a day or two, and do your best to keep track of what you are dreaming about. Here are some questions or notes you may want to track in your dream journal:

◊ How did you feel in the dream? Happy? Sad? Mystical? Curious? Anxious?

◊ Where were you in the dream? Was it a place you've been before?

◊ What was the time of day in the dream? What was the weather like?

◊ Recall one important event in the dream? Why is this event the most significant to you?

◊ Were there any numbers, colors, or names that stood out to you?

◊ Did you see anyone you know? Who is this person in your life, and how did the two of you interact?

◊ Did you hear any messages? Did you feel any premonitions or feel that you picked up information that you need to carry with you during your waking day?

DREAM INTERPRETATIONS

There are various ways to approach INTERPRETING dreams. In a modern world, finding dream interpretations can be as simple as a Google search. However, before searching the internet for all of the answers, I recommend you review what you dreamt about and create personal interpretations for yourself. In other words, how would you personally define the images you encountered in your dreams? If you dream about a cat and love cats as pets, perhaps your interpretation would be a comfortable and quiet domestic space. If you dream about cats and study magic and mythology, perhaps you would interpret it as a visit from Bast, the Egyptian cat goddess. If you dream about cats but you're allergic to them, the dream may take on a very different meaning!

Although dream dictionaries can be fantastic tools, your own perspective and background knowledge may give you the foundation you need to better understand the dream's meaning. By giving yourself the opportunity to create your own dream journal, messages and images may have a more personal and valuable meaning to you. Here is a brief list of interpretations of common dream symbols:

† AIRPLANE: A journey is nearby. To dream about missing a flight may signify feeling like you have missed an opportunity.

† ANIMALS: Animals can indicate lessons connected to spirit guides. If you dream about animals, you may want to research what they represent as spirit animals or animal totems. For example, dolphins could indicate

great communication skills, dragonflies could indicate connections to the world of the Fae, owls could indicate a time of wisdom.

† **Being Pregnant:** There is a major project that needs to be formulated and created.

† **Chases:** If you are running from a person, it could indicate running from financial fears. If you are running from monsters, you are fearful of endings. If you are running from animals, there could be delays in your life. If you are running from something you can't see, you may be running away from your feelings.

† **Crowns and Hats:** Wearing a crown or hat could indicate moving into a time where you reclaim personal power.

† **Death:** There is a major transformation or change taking place. There is an old traditional Italian belief that if you dream about someone dying, you actually add seven years to his or her life. Another old belief is that if you dream about death, someone close to you is pregnant.

† **Driving:** You are taking control of a situation or finding direction in your life.

† **Erotic Dreams:** You may be letting your desires play out, or you need to explore your desires in life (sensual or not).

† **Falling:** You feel that something is out of your control. Consider if there are any improvements you can immediately make in your life.

† **Figure 8:** To see a figure 8 could indicate a time of magical maturation.

† **FLYING:** To dream about flying indicates a desire for personal freedom and potential. Also consider what you see when you are flying in your dream.

† **FOREST:** It is a time to wander into the unknown.

† **NUDITY:** If you are naked in a dream, you are feeling vulnerable or unprepared for situations. This could also indicate a time of revealing secrets or communicating with divinity.

† **TEETH FALLING OUT:** You may have a fear or anxiety of not having control over your life. This can also be interpreted as money on the way. Let's all agree that the latter meaning sounds much more appealing!

† **WATER:** You are feeling emotional and sensitive. There can be feelings of grief or overwhelming emotions if there is a lot of water in your dream.

Dreams can be a powerful experience. They can have spiritual messages, insightful omens, and creative ideas that influence your life in a positive way. They can also help you work through challenges in your waking life and help you resolve difficult issues. Take this opportunity to work toward enhancing your dreams and following up on what you dream about to see how your dreams can shape your life for the better. Sweet dreams!

CHAPTER TWENTY

RUNES

R UNES HAVE A FASCINATING HISTORY: THEY ARE CONNECTED
to magic, myth, and the adventures of Vikings. They have been
used to dedicate stones to historic families, evoke the strength
of gods in weapons, and lead modern-day archaeologists on a trail of
where the Vikings once explored. Studying runes takes time and dedication, as well as an interest in history, archaeology, and ancient magic.
Working with runes requires a respect for Norse mythology and religions,
thus making it an enlightening and empowering experience. The runes
are a truly powerful alphabet that conjures inspiring images and deep
interpretations. Runes are a writing system, first appearing around the
2nd century CE and being used through the Medieval era. Runes were
carved into wood, horn, and stone. While mainly associated with the
Nordic region, inscriptions have been discovered all across Europe. Even
though rune shapes are relatively simple in their linear appearances, they
have far from simple interpretations. Runes function as both letters and

symbols and can spell out a word or act alone as a word. Although their origin and historical uses are often debated in the academic world, many believe runes are based on the alphabets of Mediterranean languages and older Germanic symbols.

The names of each of the runes are culturally significant: each rune letter has a name which means something significant to the cultures that created them. Some runes speak of gods, while others represent important animals. Although still debated by some runologists, there is some evidence that hints at runes holding magical significance and being used for divination. An example is the Lindholm amulet, a crescent-shaped piece of wood with a mysterious *alu* inscription on one side of it. The inscription has been found on several archaeological objects, leading many runologists to consider the amulet magical. The basic meaning of *alu* may be "ecstasy" or "magic." In *Norwegian Runes and Runic Inscriptions*, author Terje Spurkland connects the *alu* to the English word ale, noting that some scholars theorize that ale was a valuable aspect to rituals and could potentially be a protective charm (45-46). Runes may have also been used in divination by Germanic tribes through the practice of casting lots. Tacitus, a Roman writer of the first century CE, wrote about the Germanic practice of consulting omens by scratching signs into twigs.

Runes are also commonly found in Germanic mythology, the most popular being in the *Poetic Edda's* story "The Sayings of the High One." In this passage, the Norse god Odin narrates his self-sacrifice to discover the runes. After hanging from the tree of knowledge Yggdrasil for nine days, he discovers the runes and shares them with the world, describing the spells he has discovered he could use with the runes. In "Skirnir's Journey," from the *Poetic Edda*, Skirnir threatens to curse Gerd by carving three runes onto her head. In the "Lay of Sigridrifa," the Valkyrie Sigridrifa gives runic wisdom to the hero warrior Sigurd. She speaks of the *ale* rune, which may be a reference to the magical *alu* inscription.

Today, many modern Pagans and witches have rediscovered the power and magic of runes, utilizing them for divination and magic. Many people read runes to divine the future. Runes have been carved into discs or sticks of wood, painted on stones, or engraved into clay.

Try pulling one rune a day and contemplating its meaning. Perhaps you want to consider theme words to associate with the rune or meditate on. Or try pulling three runes: the first representing the past, the second representing the present, and the third representing the future. As a tarot card reader, I enjoy using runes during tarot readings. After the cards have been read, I ask the querent to take the runes and throw them over the tarot spread. Whichever runes are facedown are removed, while the runes which remain face up are read in relation to where they have fallen in the spread. Another interesting exercise is to see if you notice any runic symbols in nature. It's surprising to see how many runes appear in trees, shadows, and even architecture.

Runes have also been used as amulets to attract specific energies, as well as to enhance magic. Consider carving specific runes into candles, drawing runes on sachets or in grimoires, or wearing a rune on a piece of jewelry. Carry a rune that has energies you wish to attract into your life and see how it assists you.

Studying runes can lead you down a path of spiritual evolution. You may also find that the more you connect with runes, the more reverence you will have for the history and the ancient culture of those who first carved these deeply mystical and historical symbols. Enjoy the journey, as it will guide you toward ancient wisdom.

RUNIC ALPHABET
AND INTERPRETATIONS

There are many variations of the **RUNIC ALPHABET**, as different regions had varied letters depending on the local language. The most common standardized set of runes has twenty-four letters and is known as the common Germanic Futhark, named after the first six runic letters. Here you will find a simple overview and translations of each rune. However, it is recommended that you follow up with books from the bibliography and recommended reading at the end of this book. The name of the rune is listed, along with its corresponding letter and meaning. The divinatory meaning represents its interpretation in divination readings. There are also references in the interpretations to the Old English rune poem, a poem that was discovered in George Hickes' *Linguarum Veterum Septentrionalium Thesaurus* from 1705. Although the origin of the poem is unknown, its lyrics add intriguing imagery and depth to the runes' meanings.

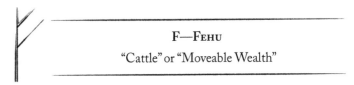

F—Fehu
"Cattle" or "Moveable Wealth"

It is the rune of wealth—abundance and prosperity have been won or earned. There is financial improvement, success, and energy. The Old English rune poem says that "Wealth is a comfort to any man/yet each person must share it out well." Thus Fehu reminds us that wealth is more than golden coins and materialism: it is how we share our abundance with others.

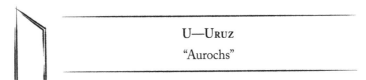

U—Uruz
"Aurochs"

Aurochs were a type of primitive cattle that youths would battle against to test their courage and skill. It is the rune of strength, energy, and good health. Success can be achieved through focus, confidence, and dedication. You are being tested—accept the challenge in front of you and personal growth will be your reward.

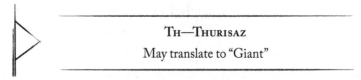

Th—Thurisaz
May translate to "Giant"

It is also known as Thor's rune, as the shape is said to resemble Thor's hammer, Mjollnir. Thurisaz is the rune of chaos, disruption, pain, catalysts, purging, and temptation. Forces out of your control create strife when Thurisaz appears. Always know what your purpose is, and do what you can to feel powerful, strong, and closer to divinity.

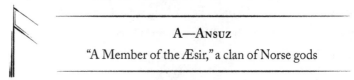

A—Ansuz
"A Member of the Æsir," a clan of Norse gods

This rune is often associated with Odin and the wisdom he shares. The Old English rune poem translates this word to "mouth." Ansuz is the rune of messages and communication. Insight, clarity, and answers are available. This appears when it is time to be expressive, to listen, to observe, to speak your truth, and to take in all available lessons through communication and speech.

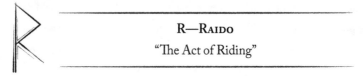

R—Raido
"The Act of Riding"

This is the rune of travel. Raido appears at a time of activity and movement. It is time to be proactive in your life. You are the one in control and the one who leads your own existence. Remember that life moves in cycles and that positive activities will take you closer to your soul's purpose. Reflect on what you have done with pride and move forward knowing you have much to give.

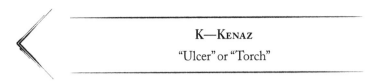

K—Kenaz
"Ulcer" or "Torch"

Kenaz is the rune of visions and is often connected to the spark of inspiration. It appears at times of creativity and transformation. It can indicate spiritual enlightenment, warm interactions with loved ones, and doing what you are inspired to do. Always do what inspires you and do not be complacent.

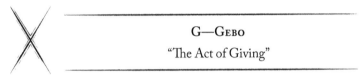

G—Gebo
"The Act of Giving"

Gebo is the rune of love, harmony, friendship, and joy. Have trust in love, work on self-love, and love for others will come naturally. Find balance between giving and receiving.

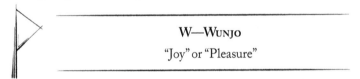

W—Wunjo
"Joy" or "Pleasure"

Wunjo is the rune of joy, pleasure, bright times, and feeling close to divinity. Consider what brings you happiness. Look for solutions as opposed to focusing on problems. It can be used in magic to manifest wishes. Use with other runes to manifest what you specifically desire.

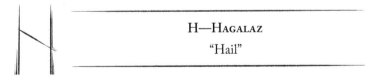

H—Hagalaz
"Hail"

Hagalaz is the rune of disruption. It appears at times of confusion and miscommunication but can lead to a phase of completion. Challenges are occurring, and it is time to face them. Listen to yourself and pay attention to what your body needs.

N—Naudiz
"Need" or "Distress."

This is the rune of necessity but also of distress, arriving in times of anxiety, delays, confusion, restrictions, and self-initiated change. When Naudiz appears, it is time to reconnect with divinity. There is a need to focus on the present moment but remain mindful that changes will eventually lead to stability and simplicity.

I—Isaz
"Ice"

This is the rune of blockages and frustration, indicating a time to turn inward. It is drawn when time feels frozen and there is a feeling of oppression. The soul desires a time of peace and quiet. Take this time to step back and realize the world is in constant motion around you. Return to a natural flow and turn inward.

J—Jera
"Year," "The Measurement of Time," and "Harvest"

This rune indicates efforts and hard work realized with abundance, hope, peace, and patience. This rune can also indicate cycles and fertility. Your garden grows and you reap what you sow.

Æ or I—Eihwaz
There is no agreement on the meaning of this rune, though it may mean "Yew Tree"

Yew was connected to protection and magic. This is the rune of transition. This marks a time for honesty and diplomacy. Stay focused in order to achieve the best end results. This can also be a time to begin planning new goals and realizing new dreams.

P—Pertho
According to the Old English rune
poem, may mean "Dice Box" or "Chessman"

Pertho is the rune of mystery and chance. It can indicate time of spiritual evolution, a time of play, or a little of both. Take chances and embrace the supernatural.

Z—Algiz
May translate to "Protection" or "Guard"

Algiz is the rune of protection. It is also associated with elk. Follow your instincts and feel the presence of the gods. There is safety if you are not reckless. Find surroundings that bring you comfort and support.

S—Sowulo
"Sun"

Sowulo is the rune of optimism and vitality, good fortune and energy. This rune appears when a positive attitude can lead to positive results. You can connect with this rune to help banish negativity, bring light to a dark situation, and use as an aid for finding your way.

T—Teiwaz
"Tyr," a god of war before Odin.

Teiwaz is the rune of the warrior, victory, success, and willingness to self-sacrifice. Have courage in your own abilities, have courage when you look in the mirror. Be diplomatic in all matters, including those that battle in your mind.

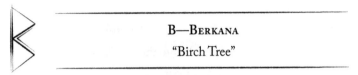

B—Berkana
"Birch Tree"

This rune is associated with fertility and springtime. Berkana is a rune of growth, purification, and fertility, marking a time of spiritual renewal, regeneration, and the promise of new beginnings. Through nurturing yourself and others, the gift of giving will spread.

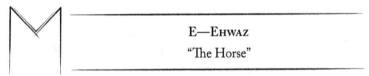

E—Ehwaz
"The Horse"

Ehwaz is the rune of momentum. The shape of this rune is thought to depict a horse's legs. Horses were sacred to the Germanic people. This is a time to avoid procrastination and laziness. Focus on steady progress, harmony, trust, and ideal partnerships. Always be willing to forgive and to not take offense.

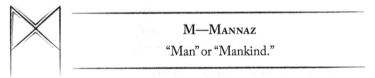

M—Mannaz
"Man" or "Mankind."

Mannaz is the rune of humanity. A time of compassion, cooperation, or assistance, as well as innocence and returning to a simple place. Contemplate your place in the world and your attitude toward others.

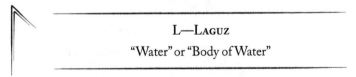

L—Laguz
"Water" or "Body of Water"

This Rune can be connected to rituals in water or voyages. Laguz can indicate confusion and a need for quietness to hear intuitive guidance.

Follow your intuition and contemplate what "going with the flow" feels like to you. Laguz can also indicate an inward journey where you explore your own inner depths for awareness.

NG—INGUZ
"Fertility God, counterpart to the Mother Goddess"

Inguz is a reference to a fertility god who was a Green Man, a counterpart to the Mother Goddess, and a divine hero. It is the rune of peace. It indicates a time when all tasks are completed and there is a stage of rest. Grow closer to nature to feel a oneness with divinity.

D—DAGAZ
"Day" or "Daylight"

Dagaz is the rune of transformation. A rune of hope, release, happiness, and certainty. Believe in yourself and that you can have the best for yourself. Life will give you what you ask for.

O—OTHILA
"Inherited Wealth," "Homeland," and "Family Estate."

Othila is the rune of family, safety, increase, and abundance. A time to reconnect with loved ones and spirituality. Share without boundaries— share wealth, knowledge, and love, and you will be rewarded.

EXPLORING THE DIVINE
NATURE OF RUNES WITH MS. KATHRYN

Ms. Kathryn is a divination expert with a heathen background and thirty-five years of experience in eclectic witchcraft. She is an intuitive spiritual reader of runes, cards, and bones in the French Quarter of New Orleans. She has long been devoted to the study and wisdom of runic knowledge and all divination. She felt particularly drawn to her Norse ancestry at a young age:

"In my early twenties, a fellow witch sister gifted me Freya Aswyn's book, *Northern Mysteries and Magick: Runes & Feminine Powers* complete with a CD of Rune galdr. I found my path and the runes awakened the seer within me."

Ms. Kathryn has devoted daily practice to working with the runes and through this connects with them deeply. She actually practices *stadr*, a runic yoga. In addition to this, she maintains daily meditation, journaling, vision boards, manifestation work, and shadow work. The runes even support her family dynamics.

Her entire back is tattooed with runes that say health, family, courage, and honor: "It is the code by which I raised my three sons as a single mother. To this day, my sons who are now grown men can recite our family code."

She encourages those who are curious about studying runes to dive into Norse culture and mythology. She also feels deeply aligned with the feminine powers of runes, noting how magical the feminine Norns of fate are: "Our spiritual blood already contains the knowledge of the runes in it. We just have to tap into that natural power."

Ms. Kathryn makes it very clear that runes are incredibly powerful and require dedication and practice. Working with runes isn't just a divination system; it's a spiritual gift that requires study and dedication: "With every reading, you are essentially descending into yourself, your shadow, your subconscious so you can rise to your higher self with the help of runic power. Runes love to give homework. They can be quite the task master."

CHAPTER TWENTY-ONE

SCRYING

YOU MAY ALREADY BE FAMILIAR WITH WHAT SCRYING is, even if you are unfamiliar with the term itself. Imagine the stereotypical image of a woman dressed in scarves and jewelry, gazing into a shiny crystal ball with the hopes of seeing a vision of the future. This act of gazing is scrying, though perhaps the modern-day scrying scene is a little less theatrical.

Scrying is a form of divination that utilizes the art of gazing into a reflective surface to try to achieve psychic impressions. For some, scrying can help shift the mind into a trance-like state in which psychic messages are easily received in the form of images, symbols, and feelings. This is a form of divination that will come up again and again. People use mirrors, water, and even fire for scrying. For right now, however, let's look more closely at the basic ways you can practice scrying.

HISTORY OF SCRYING

The HISTORY OF SCRYING is a vast one. Cultures from around the world used scrying as a means of gaining psychic information. Ancient societies, such as those of Mesopotamia, Greece, Rome, and Celtic Ireland, practiced scrying. It is a method of divination that has continued throughout history, influencing some of the greatest esoteric minds. The legendary alchemist John Dee claimed to have used a crystal ball to communicate with angels in the late sixteenth century, and, as a result of his practice, he gained knowledge of the angelic Enochian alphabet and language. Nostradamus was said to have used scrying to predict future lineage of the kings of France for Queen Catherine de' Medici.

WHAT TO USE FOR SCRYING

Many SCRYERS have depended on crystal balls or blackened mirrors to scry. Crystal spheres and mirrors are a staple item at metaphysical shops—obsidian or jet are favored crystals for scrying because of their dark, shiny surfaces. You can, however, practice scrying without a store-bought item if you would like. Some people choose to carefully stare into the flame of a small spell candle, whereas some prefer to use the reflective surface of water to scry. You will find more scrying information in the fire divination section (page 99) and the forest divination section (page 111) of this book.

PREPARATION FOR
SCRYING AND HOW TO SCRY

There are a variety of ways to set up an area for OPTIMAL scrying, though experimenting in a setup that is uniquely comfortable and optimal for you will take practice. Be sure that you will not be disturbed by outside distractions in this space. Prepare a clean, comfortable, and darkened space to scry in—the room can have a traditional protective circle of salt, it can be decorated with crystals, or it can have incense burning, if those are things you would like to add to your space. You may want to cleanse before and after your sessions to clear energy as well.

The method I have found to be most functional is as follows. Set up your scrying instrument (crystal ball, bowl, or mirror) on a table in front of you. Use two candles on the sides of the instrument. Some people prefer just one candle, though you can play around with this to see what works best for you. Arrange the candles so the surface has a glow of light but does not show a mirror reflection of yourself—you do not want to be staring at yourself for the entire scrying session. Close your eyes for a moment to ground and center yourself. Use this time to recite a mantra or prayer, connect with spirit guides, or focus your intentions on a question you would like to examine during your scrying session. When you open your eyes, gaze into the surface of the scrying instrument. "Un-focus" your eyes and lean into the feeling of "staring into space." Quiet your mind by focusing on your breath. Scrying sessions are generally between five and twenty minutes long. When you first begin, keep your sessions shorter, and continually increase the amount of time you scry as you see fit.

WHAT TO EXPECT FROM SCRYING

The big question asked in regard to scrying is "WHAT AM I GOING TO SEE?" Results differ from scryer to scryer and from session to session. Some scryers say they will see actual images in the surface. Perhaps their eyes experience a moment of "matrixing," during which a shape seen in the surface is reclassified in their mind as something they're already familiar with. Some say they see nothing at all but instead experience a very calming and meditative session in which they are able to escape the "hamster's running wheel" feeling in their mind, coming out of the session feeling refreshed, Zen, or inspired. Others say they see the scrying tool's surface fill with what appears to be clouds or smoke. Instead of looking for something, perhaps it is worth noticing how you feel or what you hear. Much like dream interpretations, scrying interpretations tend to be personal, based on personal experiences and associations with certain symbols and images. Through practice and journaling, you can begin to develop a sense of what certain images, sounds, and feelings indicate or represent. Journaling will also allow you the valuable opportunity to reflect on past sessions to see if anything has come to pass.

CHAPTER TWENTY-TWO

SEASHELL DIVINATION

T HE BEACH IS A MAGICAL SANCTUARY FOR ME. It is a healing experience, both emotionally and physically. I think many people will agree that a visit to the ocean can be a spiritual and magical experience as well; there is something mystical and wondrous about the ocean. One of my all-time favorite activities is beach combing, that is the act of searching the sand for shells and other special objects like sand dollars and shark teeth. Walking on the beach is a form of meditation for me—a mindful walk on the beach looking for treasures along the shore with the waves reaching into the soft sands. I know I am not the first to use shells in divination, nor am I the first to suggest a method for using them in divination. This seashell divination kit is truly personal, and I am sharing it with you so you can see how much is possible with divination.

I feel that my seashell kit is similar to my bone and trinket kit, since they both contain precious objects that once held life. If you're interested in using seashells for divination, start by collecting special and unique shells. Your own shell kit will be unique to you. You can collect shells from various beaches, from different locations or vacations, or as gifts from other people. Perhaps the energy of different locations or memories remain with the shells and could then help you in your interpretations for what each of the shells symbolize. You may even find there are other sea treasures that you want to add: sea glass, coral, stones, and so on. I recommend selecting items that are all similar in size and not fragile like sea stars or crab shells. Also, be mindful to examine what you've collected and be sure there are no signs of life, like hermit crabs for example. When you have all of your shells gathered, keep them in a safe container—a small, lined box or a soft pouch would be perfect.

The next step is figuring out what each of the shells represent in your kit. Each shell will signify a unique interpretation and you can consider themes that are important to you. You can make your kit simple and small or more complex and constantly evolving. You will find that some will be theme shells, whereas others will be action shells. Where they land in your reading will help you to create a story and determine priorities, as well as where actions need to take place.

On the following pages is a list of shells in my personal kit, so you can see the different assignments I gave to my shells. Part of the fun in this project was learning how to identify different shells at my local beach, another fun activity for a researcher at heart.

MY PERSONAL SHELL KIT

† Sun Shell: Orange Ark Shell. A ribbed, clam-shaped shell, this one represents the way you feel in the world around you, how you want the world to see you, along with goals, success, and ambitions.

† Wealth Shell: White Ark Shell. This shell represents money, success, prosperity, and career.

† Challenge Shell: Black Ark Shell. This shell represents where there are challenges and opportunities for improvement.

† Moon Shell: Moon Snail Shell. This large, spiraled shell is for emotional urges, dreams, intuition, and psychic abilities. This represents the forces of the moon and the internal world.

† Change Shell: Black Olive Shell. A sturdy, cylindrical shell, this represents where there is change in your life.

† Responsibility Shell: Brown Olive Shell. This shell represents going into a period of hard work and extensive efforts to push to the finish line. There is a need to focus on responsibilities to get things done in order to see results.

† Creativity Shell: Orange Olive Shell. This shell represents self-expression, artistic pursuits, and creative ideas worth manifesting in reality.

† Mystery Shell: Black Jingle Clam. A shiny shell also known as *Anomia*, this is the "wild shell," which represents magical influences, fate, divine intervention, curious developments, and where to make mindful observations of the world around you.

† Success Shell: White Jingle Clam. This shell represents where things are going well and can indicate good news.

† **Health Shell:** Blue Auger. A spire-shaped shell, this represents health, healing, and physical wellness.

† **Knowledge Shell:** Orange Auger. This shell represents what to study or something to focus on learning and mastering.

† **Self-Care Shell:** White Baby's Ear. A gentle, ear-shaped shell with a spiral pattern, this represents what you need to focus on and care for in your life, as well as where you need to be more forgiving and tender with yourself.

† **Love Shell:** Orange Baby's Ear. This shell represents love, romance, romantic relationships, and romantic partners.

† **Meditation Shell:** Purple & White Dwarf Surf Clam. A soft, fanned-out shell, this is the shell that represents where you need to pause, go inward, and contemplate. It is about non-action.

† **Home Shell:** Ribbed Cantharus. A white textured conch-shaped shell, this represents stability, the homestead, family, and where there is comfort.

† **Adventure Shell:** Lightning Whelk. A smooth conch-shaped shell with orange stripes, this shell represents travel, journey, and what needs to be explored. It is where you can take risks and make great strides.

† **Atlantis Shell:** Cerith Shell. A spiral-shaped, this one looks like a cross between the auger and the cantharus. This shell represents having ties to past lives with the wonderful Mother Ocean. To receive this shell shows a special tie to the ocean and hearing its calling.

† **Surprise Shell:** Iridescent Oyster. A small piece of lovely, rainbow-colored, iridescent oyster shell, this represents receiving an unexpected gift, a rare opportunity, a unique interaction, or a surprise encounter.

† **Introvert Shell:** Eastern White Slippersnail. A flat, textured white shell with what looks like a pocket on the inside, this shell represents a time of retreating inward and celebrating gentle and quiet contemplation, observation, and deep thinking.

† **Extrovert Shell:** Tulip Snail Shell. A shell shaped like a spire, this one suggests getting out into the world, socializing, networking, and doing activities that boost your energy and endurance. This highlights the need to explore what is fun for the querent.

† **Faith Shell:** Angel Wing Shell. A piece of the gentle and white shell that looks like a feathered wing, this one represents hope, faith, and willpower.

† **Mermaid Shell:** Lucine Shell. A white shell with cross hatches across the surface, this represents beauty and the spirit of the ocean. It can indicate a connection to the element of water or a calling to visit the ocean.

To cast the shells, you will need to create a space where you can throw them carefully. If you are on the beach, it is as simple as drawing a circle in the sand and using that area to cast in. If you are not on the beach, you may want to consider creating a special circular piece of fabric, such as a piece of velvet. Or, if you are a playful beach bum, why not even use a repurposed beach towel? This is up to you. Draw the circle and put a cross through it, dividing it into four sections. Anything that lands in the top half of the circle represents outside influences; this could indicate other people and situations that are outside of your own. Anything that lands in the bottom half of the circle represents what is going on within your own life, indicating things that shape your world and that you have control over. Anything that lands on the left side of the circle represents the past; anything in the center represents priorities and present concerns; and anything in the right part of the circle represents future events.

Take the shells and hold them in your hands—if you are reading for someone else, ask them to do the same. Take a moment to center and connect with the shells, knowing they represent the intuitive power and vast magic of the ocean. Think about what is most important to you at the moment—where you need direction, support, or advice. When you are ready, gently throw the shells into the circle. If any land outside of the circle, you do not need to use them in the reading: just focus on what is inside the circle. Examine where the shells land. Which shells sit close to each other? Where are they in the circle? Use the meanings of the shells to guide what has happened, what is happening currently, and what is going to happen in the future.

SAMPLE SHELL READING

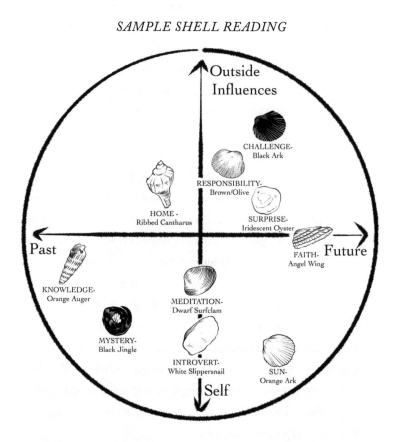

The question for this sample shell reading is "What can I do to improve my love life?" Many shells fell within this circle, and to make it easier to decipher, see the above interpretation of each shell in the diagram.

Looking at this reading, it is interesting to see two different stories taking place in the person's life, as well as the outer influences. The person getting this reading looks like they came into some information; since this is a love reading, the knowledge obtained must have something to do with the suitor in question, who is going through a very different experience. The person getting the reading looks like they are on an internal journey: the mystery, meditation, and introvert shells indicate that, while it is tempting to focus on looking for love from others, the best relationship to focus on at the current moment is the self. Through meditation and spiritual work, there will be a lot of success and personal growth. This personal growth and development will put the person in the right frame of mind to connect with the suitor.

The suitor, on the other hand, identified by the shells in the outside influences area of the circle, is tied to responsibilities at home. Instead of being able to go inward, the suitor is working at home or has tasks at hand that do not allow them to focus on love life. Looking at these shells, I would even suggest that someone at home may need caregiving or extra support, and the suitor has taken on the role of caregiver. However, a challenging and surprising event occurs for the suitor—to me it looks like a change in roles. The suitor's allowed to finally look at love again, and the faith shell shows that the two can finally meet at the right time.

How would you interpret this shell reading?

CHAPTER TWENTY-THREE

SELENOMANCY:

Moon Divination

S ELENOMANCY IS THE TERM FOR DIVINATION BY THE moon's appearance. While you are outdoors celebrating the magic of the moon, consider trying divination with it! As with many natural forms of divination, the light of the moon can be used to scry in the surface of water. During a full moon, go to a quiet place where you can look into a body of water; for example, a lake, river, or perhaps even a bird bath in a garden. Stare into the ripples of the water, allowing the reflection and light of the moon to relax you.

The way you view the moon can be an indicator of fortunes ahead of you:

◊ If you first see the new moon sliver in front of you or to your right, you will have a good month. If you first see it to your left or have to turn around to see it, you will have a difficult month.

◊ Do not look at a full moon over your left shoulder, as this could bring bad luck. Instead, look at the full moon over your right shoulder.

A few noted folklore traditions about divining for love with the moon:
◊ A red ring around the moon means someone has fallen in love.
◊ An Old Welsh tradition told women to look at the first full moon of the new year through a silk handkerchief. The number of moons she'd see through the silk veil would reveal the number of months she would remain unmarried.
◊ *The Encyclopedia of Superstitions, Folklore, and the Occult Sciences of the World, Vol. 2* shares an old saying to announce under a new moon to help foretell of a future partner: "New moon, new, tell me true / Who my husband will be. / The clothes he will wear the color of his hair / And the happy day he will wed me" (964).

There are also plenty of omens about the weather based on the moon. If weather omens are of interest to you, consider getting an annual copy of the *Farmers' Almanac*, a great source for folklore predictions about weather surrounding the moon and astrology. A few such weather predictions based on the moon are as follows:
◊ "Clear moon, frost soon." A clear night when you can see the moon and the stars means that cloud cover cannot keep heat in. It is possible that you are seeing a cooler and crisper evening if you can look up and see the moon.
◊ Two moons in a month could indicate flooding.
◊ A full moon on Christmas means a bad harvest.
◊ If you see a moon with the crescent pointing upward, it will not rain.
◊ If you see a moon with the crescent pointing downward, it will rain.
◊ An Irish folklore belief says that a yellow halo around the moon can indicate incoming wet weather.
◊ There is an old saying that says, "The bigger the ring, the bigger the wet."

◊ Rainy and windy weather is said to follow a new moon on a Saturday.

◊ If the moon looks pale, rain will follow.

◊ When the "horns" of the crescent moon look sharp, it will rain the next day, or there will be frost if it is winter.

Scott Cunningham has a mysterious moon divination to try at the full moon in his book *The Art of Divination*. On the new moon, go outside and point a dull-bladed silver knife at the moon. Say the following incantation: "New moon, true morrow, be true now to me/That I ere the morrow my true love may see." Speak to no one as you get ready for bed and place the knife under your pillow. Cunningham simply says, "Remember your dreams," (97). Perhaps this means the dreams will offer images and omens of things to come.

PSYCHIC POTION FOR THE MOON

The moon can be used to assist in psychic magic. For many, plants, herbs, and oils associated with the moon can be used in magic that is meant to enhance psychic abilities and intuitive awareness. This is an oil you can make for when you want to enhance your psychic abilities or have vivid dreams with psychic messages. You can also anoint your divination tools with this blend or wear it when you are performing divination. The following recipe is meant for a four-dram bottle. Please note that I use diluted forms of jasmine and sandalwood essential oils. Note that this is not for internal use: do not consume!

- 21 DROPS SANDALWOOD
- 13 DROPS JASMINE
- 9 DROPS BLUE LOTUS
- 9 DROPS VANILLA
- 1 DROP LEMON
- 1 DROP LEMONGRASS

OPTIONAL: Add moonstone chips, myrrh resin, and dried yarow to this. You may also add gardenia or coconut fragrance oils if you like.

MOON MAGIC AND PSYCHIC
WORK WITH MICHAEL HERKES

Michael Herkes lives in Chicago and is best known as "The Glam Witch" and is a devotee to the goddess Lilith. He focuses his practice on crystal, glamour, moon, and sex magic. He is also an experienced tarot reader, speaker, and author of *The GLAM Witch: The Complete Book of Moon Spells*, as well as a contributor to *Witch Way Magazine*.

Because of his work with moon magic, I asked him to share how honoring the moon has influenced his magical practice and psychic work. He has always felt drawn to the moon, contemplating the numerological significance of his date of birth, the 18th, and The Moon card in tarot.

Michael has worked with a variety of divination forms. He has been most drawn tarot, feeling that his intuition is heightened by the symbolism and art in the cards. He also works with scrying, which is much like a ritual for him: "I also do scrying from time to time, with a black obsidian mirror, crystal ball, or my favorite way—to draw a bath by candlelight with a black bath bomb. I use the black waters to scry and find it very powerful to be submerged in the water, especially considering the moon's gravitational pull that controls the tides."

While he works with divination at all phases of the moon, he notes that the supermoons are potent times for him to perform divination:

"Supermoons occur when a new or full moon's orbit is closest to Earth. Eclipses are another powerful time, as they symbolize the blending of solar and lunar energy." He suggests that divination practitioners learn about their moon sign as well: "Every two to three days, the moon enters another zodiac sign. You will be most connected to the moon when it is in the same sign as your natal moon sign, making it a potent time to work with lunar energy."

He sleeps with labradorite under his pillow, which helps him have vivid dreams, especially during the full moon. He also has advice for those interested in working with the moon: "I would recommend not trying to look at the moon as a monthly event, avoiding putting an emphasis on the new or full phases over the others. The moon is always full, always whole, and always around. We don't have to see it to know that it is there. It is continuously changing and transforming—just like witchcraft."

CHAPTER TWENTY-FOUR

STONE AND CRYSTAL DIVINATION

S TICKS AND STONES MAY BREAK BONES, BUT THEY can also help you see the future. Stone divination sets are easy to put together and use. They are short, sweet, and discreet. They can be helpful on their own, or they can be used along with other divination readings.

URIM AND THUMMIM

Turning to STONES for divination is not a new idea. This practice was used in the Old Testament of the Bible by priests who carried two stones in their breastplates. These stones were called URIM, meaning "light," and THUMMIM, meaning "perfection." Priests would use these two stones to find answers to questions.

CREATING SIMPLE STONE SETS:
TWO AND THREE-STONE VARIATIONS

† **Twon-Stone Set:** For a Two-Stone Set, get two very similarly shaped stones. Oftentimes, people will get one white stone to signify "yes" and one black stone to signify "no." If you want to use different colors you can. Keep both stones in a bag, and when you have a question hold the bag. With your eyes closed, pull one stone out to receive your answer.

† **Three-Stone Set:** For a Three-Stone Set, get three very similarly shaped stones. One stone should be light in color to signify "yes," one should be dark to signify "no," and the third should be a color of your choice for the "significator," representing the person receiving the reading. Hold the three stones in your hands and think of your question, then roll the stones onto a table. The stone that sits closest to the significator indicates the answer.

SIX-STONE VARIATION

This is the version I learned a long time ago. Unfortunately, I do not have any resources for this variation, since it was taught to me in a class, but it has worked well for me over the years. I will sometimes have people in tarot readings pull from this set if they are interested.

† **Six-Stone Set:** You will need six small stones that are similar in shape and size. Three of these stones should three light or white stones to indicate "yes" and the other three dark or black stones to indicate "no." Keep them together in a small pouch. Think about your question while holding the pouch with the stones inside. Pull three stones. Three white stones indicate "yes, definitely"; two white stones and one black indicate "most likely"; two black stones and one white indicate "probably not"; and three black stones indicate "definitely not."

FIFTY-STONES VARIATION

In *Cunningham's Encyclopedia of Crystal, Gem and Metal Magic*, author Scott Cunningham suggests a fun version of simple stone divination. Collect a bowl full of tumbled crystals and smooth stones that are similar in size. Whenever you have a question, grab a handful of the crystals from the bowl. If you pull an odd number of stones, your answer is favorable, positive, or successful. If you pull an even number of stones, your answer is unfavorable, negative, or perhaps not so fortunate.

PESSOMANCY

PESSOMANCY, sometimes known as psephomancy, is the divination of pebbles or beans. This was a popular form of divination in Ancient Greece. For some, the collection of pebbles is thrown onto the ground and the forms they make on the ground will determine the omen. For others, the pebbles have symbols marked on them to signify different matters, such as health, career, and love. The symbols and shapes made can then be interpreted. To try a simple version of pessomancy, collect many small pebbles or beans and place them in a basket or bag. When you have a question, shake the pebbles around and cast them onto the ground. Interpret the shapes and patterns made by the pebbles, much like you would for divining tea leaves.

LITHOMANCY

LITHOMANCY comes from Greek, with *lithos* meaning "stone" and *mancy* meaning "divination." It is the casting or scrying of precious stones, crystals, and gems. Stone-casting divination traditionally uses thirteen stones pulled from a pouch and released onto an area that is divided into various sections with different meanings. The exciting aspect of lithomancy is that you can follow a very traditional system of reading crystals and stones, or you can create your own system based on what works best for you.

TRADITIONAL LITHOMANCY

There are thirteen stones in a **TRADITIONAL LITHOMANCY** set. They are separated into two categories: personal stones and planetary stones. The personal stones represent your life and the people in it, and the planetary stones follow astrological interpretations. It is recommended that you pick stones and crystals that you are drawn to; however, there are suggestions in the following list of interpretations based on the astrological correspondences of crystals. Please note that the stone names listed here come from the comprehensive book *Lithomancy: The Psychic Art of Reading Stones*, by Gary L. Wimmer. Some people make variations on the personal stones. I have seen lists that include spirit, earth, fire, water, and air, while other lists have universe, news, and luck stones. I am following Wimmer's guide because it is the most extensive.

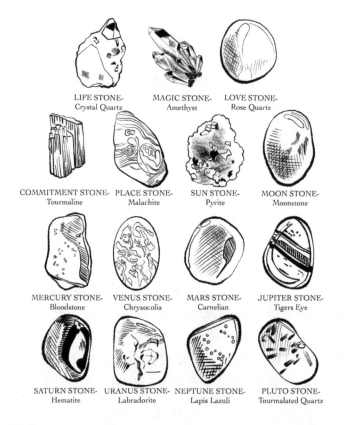

LIFE STONE-
Crystal Quartz

MAGIC STONE-
Amethyst

LOVE STONE-
Rose Quartz

COMMITMENT STONE-
Tourmaline

PLACE STONE-
Malachite

SUN STONE-
Pyrite

MOON STONE-
Moonstone

MERCURY STONE-
Bloodstone

VENUS STONE-
Chrysocolia

MARS STONE-
Carnelian

JUPITER STONE-
Tigers Eye

SATURN STONE-
Hematite

URANUS STONE-
Labradorite

NEPTUNE STONE-
Lapis Lazuli

PLUTO STONE-
Tourmalated Quartz

† **LIFE STONE:** The life stone represents the subject's valuable matters at hand. This can include the subject's thoughts, activities, support systems, and ideas. Think of this stone as representing the guiding forces for the subject and that its interpretation can be further understood by seeing where it lands and what is around it.

† **MAGIC STONE:** The magic stone represents events that are happening to help you. This stone can represent events that feel like fate or magical moments that assist and guide the subject.

† **LOVE STONE:** The love stone represents love and romantic patterns in the subject's life. It can represent loved ones, family, relationships, and emotional attachments.

† **COMMITMENT STONE:** The commitment stone represents matters that need to be taken care of. It indicates obligations and responsibilities that shape the subject's day-to-day life.

† **PLACE STONE:** The place stone represents places of security for the subject. This can be their home or other places that offer safety and comfort.

† **SUN STONE:** The Sun Stone represents your unique personality. It represents confidence, empowerment, development of courage and self-esteem, and father figures. The Sun Stone asks you to consider: what are your ambitions? Who inspires you? Who do you inspire? How do you influence others in a positive way? *Suggested crystals*: amber, sunstone, orange calcite, and pyrite.

† **MOON STONE:** The Moon Stone represents emotions, dreams, imagination, home, health, moods, receptivity, intuition, and mother figures. The Moon Stone asks you to consider: what have your dreams been telling

you to do? How do you rest, relax, and heal? Where do you feel safe and secure? *Suggested crystals*: moonstone, selenite, and pearl.

† **MERCURY STONE:** The Mercury Stone represents communication, intellect, travel, energy, knowledge, study, flexibility, energy, information, honesty, and siblings. The Mercury Stone asks you to consider: are you being honest with yourself and others? What do you need to study or become skilled at? What journey will lead you to a better place? *Suggested crystals*: aventurine, bloodstone, mica, and pumice.

† **VENUS STONE:** The Venus Stone represents beauty, love, fertility, sensuality, romance, partnership, culture, art, poetry, happiness, leisure, creativity, peace, forgiveness, femininity, and social activity. The Venus Stone asks you to consider: which relationships bring pleasure to your life? Which artistic pursuits bring you joy? How can you develop hope and kindness? *Suggested crystals*: pink tourmaline, chrysocolla, emerald, and turquoise.

† **MARS STONE:** The Mars Stone represents ambition, determination, competition, expansion, personal power, assertion, decisions, endurance, courage, and masculinity. The Mars Stone asks you to consider: when do you have to show courage? What aspect of your life can you be more proactive in? How do you keep anger and jealousy in check? *Suggested crystals*: garnet, red jasper, ruby, flint, and carnelian.

† **JUPITER STONE:** The Jupiter Stone represents aspirations, luck, generosity, opportunity, abundance, indulgences, expansion, morality, and law. The Jupiter stone asks you to consider: where can you be more open minded? What are you grateful for in your life? What are your goals for growth? *Suggested crystals*: tiger's eye, lepidolite, and topaz

† **SATURN STONE:** The Saturn Stone represents responsibility, delays,

limitations, restrictions, discipline, organization, focus, perseverance, and authority figures. The Saturn Stone asks you to consider: what needs better organization or structure in your life? How do you stay focused and optimistic? How do you respond to stress? *Suggested crystals*: jet, obsidian, hematite, and coal. Wimmer adds in the planets (including Pluto) to make a collection of sixteen stones total:

† **URANUS STONE:** The Uranus Stone represents originality, rebellion, eccentricity, bohemianism, enlightenment, connections to the occult, mystery, invention, and friendship. The Uranus Stone asks you to consider: where do you feel the most free and independent? How is your uniqueness a personality strength? How do you honor your flashes of insight? *Suggested crystals*: opal, labradorite, and fluorite.

† **NEPTUNE STONE:** The Neptune Stone represents spirituality, empathy, art, delusion, abstract ideas, introspection, psychic abilities, charisma, and deception. The Neptune Stone asks you to consider: how do you practice spirituality? How do you connect with divinity? Are you trying to avoid your problems? Are you craving time alone for reflection? *Suggested crystals*: amethyst, celestite, kyanite, and lapis lazuli.

† **PLUTO STONE:** The Pluto Stone represents change, transition, rebirth, purpose, values, secrets, profound thoughts or revelations, potential, redemption, and psychology. The Pluto Stone asks you to consider: how do you respond to change? What needs to be reevaluated in your life? Are you open to deeply spiritual or challenging revelations? *Suggested crystals*: tourmaline quartz and moldavite.

The traditional method of reading crystals and stones seems to have very few guidelines and is left to the reader's interpretation. Create an area for the stones to be cast using a long string or ribbon, then throw the stones into the circle. Interpret readings based on where the stones land and where they land in relation to each other. Do you see any shapes made from certain stones? Perhaps seeing a heart shape indicates a need to focus on love or a line of stones indicates needing to stay on target. Are there stones pointing at one other? Perhaps these stones are important solutions or advice for each other. Are they all near each other? This could indicate strong relationships. Let your intuition help you determine which patterns have certain meanings.

You may want to consider mapping out your own "mat" or "guide" to throw the stones on. If you enjoy the astrological aspects of lithomancy, create a circular map that shows the astrological houses, basing the interpretations on where the stones land. Or, if you'd like, create a map that follows the Wheel of the Year to predict seasons or energies based on the eight sabbats. You may wish to throw the stones on top of tarot or oracle cards to add another layer to a card reading. Get creative, and remember that lithomancy takes study, intuitive practice, and self-reflection for long-term success.

CREATING YOUR OWN SET &
KIKI'S LITHOMANCY CRYSTAL SET

While some people feel it is necessary to follow the traditional guidelines for lithomancy, others like to create their own parameters, determining their own meanings for specific stones and crystals, as well as using varying numbers of crystals. You can use fancy crystals, pebbles you find on walks, or even include small trinkets that are not stones. You can create a simple or complex system of lithomancy, one that has few stones or many, one that involves casting stones onto a map or one that involves pulling a couple of stones with a message.

I have fallen in love with my crystal divination kit and now find it to be one of my preferred divination tools to work with. While my kit loosely follows the parameters suggested by Wimmer, I have added many additional crystals, all of which over time have developed their own interpretations and meanings. I have also found that adding unique and special stones that I've collected from places I've visited have given it deeper meaning. I am sharing with you the current contents of my crystal divination kit, along with some brief themes and interpretations that are raised when these crystals appear in the reading.

LIFE STONE – *Kambacha Jasper* – significant events, powerful moments, priorities and focus points

MAGIC STONE – *Blue/White Crystal* – divinity, magical talents, fate, enchantment, invisible forces at work

LOVE STONE – *Rose Quartz* – partnership, emotional connections, deep feelings

COMMITMENT STONE – *Dalmation Jasper* – responsibilities, obligations, goals and promises that need to be followed through to completion

PLACE STONE – *Flat River Rock* – places of power, a place's meaning, or location

SUN STONE – *Sunstone* – where you are developing in the world, goals, personal charm, success, opportunity for growth

MOON STONE – *Moonstone* – where you are developing internally, rest, dreams, moods, opportunity to connect with inner feelings

MERCURY STONE – *Hypersthene* – where you need to speak up, travel, motion (both physical and metaphorical), things to examine closely and research fervently

Venus Stone – *Emerald* – romantic love if near love stone, self-love if near sun stone, places where devotion and authentic feelings are prevalent

Mars Stone – *Carnelian* – situations that you need to be active in, where you are learning strength and determination, lessons in courage and empowerment

Jupiter Stone – *Tiger's Eye* – where you have luck on your side, things to be grateful for, expansion and opportunities

Saturn Stone – *Obsidian* – challenges, setbacks, limitations, and where you will need to persist and persevere

Uranus Stone – *Labradorite* – your uniqueness, your personal mojo, moments of enlightenment, where to practice individuality

Neptune Stone – *Lapis Lazuli* – your spirituality, spiritual practices you can focus on for support and personal development, where to ask for divine help, spirit guides, psychic premonitions

Pluto Stone – *Tourmaline Quartz* – transition, change, revelations, complete change that help you grow and do better

Health Stone – *Moss Agate* – physical, spiritual, or mental health, depending on what stones it sits nearby

Prosperity Stone – *Pyrite* – money, success, prosperity

Truth Stone – *Trulite* – where you need to be more honest, where a mirror of truth is being held up for closer examination

ANCIENTS STONE – *Crystal from Caracol, Belize* – profound spiritual practices of the world around us, mysteries and secrets of sacred sites and practices, a connection to our spiritual past

FAE STONE – *Fluorite* – a connection to the otherworld, hedge witchcraft, a need to connect with nature

INSPIRATION STONE – *Honey Calcite* – creativity, artistic projects, expression of the imagination

STILLNESS STONE – *Sodalite* – pause, quiet, introspection, non-action

ENLIGHTENED STONE – *Citrine* – meditation, chanting, mantras, finding creative inspiration in joyously observing all around you

GUARDIAN STONE – *Malachite* – The stone of protection, the stone where you are guarded or where your spirit guides come into your life

PURITY STONE – *Shell Fossil* – a stone of authenticity, simplicity, and the removal of complication

WITCH'S STONE – *Hagstone* – your magic and witchcraft, what makes you magical, your personal mojo

STAR CHILD STONE – *Sugilite* – your connection to the universe, your ancestry in the stars, your connection to a universal community, higher dimensions

SEA STONE – waves of emotions or events, going with the flow, tides in and tides out

Siberian Blue Quartz – your influence, how you inspire others, your soul's purpose, your soul's desires

SAMPLE READING WITH CRYSTAL SET

For this crystal reading, I did a general reading using a circular mat with the twelve astrological houses charted. I asked the person to go through the crystals and select the ones they liked. They then gently dropped them over the circle. Those that remained in the circle are charted in the diagram for the reading. If you need a refresher on what each of the astrological houses mean, go back to the astrology section of this book.

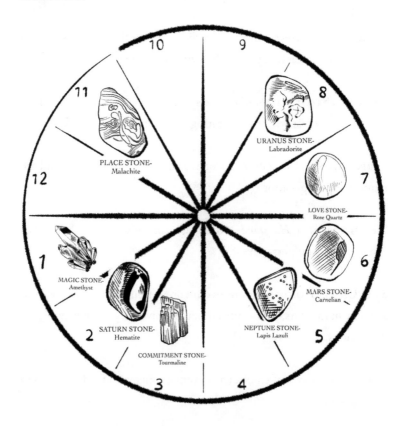

Seeing the magical stone in the First House would indicate having a present focus on magic and mysticism. This person feels they are in a magical space.

Seeing the Saturn stone in the Second House would indicate possibly having some financial setbacks or challenges. Perhaps they can use their magic to help in supporting this or asking a partner for support. Since the love stone is in the Seventh House, I would assume there's a healthy partnership.

Seeing the commitment stone in the Third House would lead me to ask what types of commitments they have to relatives. Do they feel they have responsibilities or goals that are regarding study and communication? Perhaps they are goals that are involved with elevating magical talents.

Seeing the Neptune stone in the Fifth House would indicate hobbies and creative endeavors tied to spirituality. Perhaps this person should find activities that both simultaneously bring them joy and spiritual progression. With seeing the Uranus stone in the Eighth House of the occult, I would suggest divination as a practice to take up.

There are two delightful stones in the Seventh House of partnerships: the love stone and the truth stone. This to me would indicate that there is a healthy partnership—it looks like this person has found true love and may even be someone who they can enjoy these magical and spiritual pursuits with.

The Eighth House of transformation and the occult has the Uranus stone in it. Transformation leads to uniqueness in this person, and perhaps this is a place that can assist in resolving the financial woes of the Saturn stone.

Finally, the guardian stone is in the Eleventh House of friendship and humanitarianism. It is a profound placement for spiritual protection. Perhaps this person feels safe and secure in knowing they have strong friendships around them. Or perhaps they can call upon their spirit guides for magical support in community work.

In general, this is a spiritual person who is deeply devoted to spiritual pursuits and personal transformation. They would benefit from working with other like-minded individuals and finding fun activities to deepen their spirituality. While there may be some financial setbacks, this reading would indicate that things are being put into place to help support them out of those challenges, whether it is creating a strong commitment to fixing those problems or asking that wonderful and loving partner for a little help.

CHAPTER TWENTY-FIVE

TASSEOGRAPHY:

Reading Tea Leaves

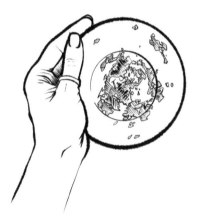

TEA-LEAF READINGS CAN BE AN INTRICATE AND EXTENSIVE form of divination. Known as tasseography, this is an old and well-loved divination technique of reading by interpreting the shapes and patterns of tea leaves in the bottom of a teacup. You will need a traditional teacup—the less of an angle on the sides, the better. In other words, you do not want a coffee mug but a cup with plenty of surface for the leaves to remain on the sides, as well as at the bottom of the cup.

DIVINATION
WITH TEA LEAVES

Begin by placing a teaspoon of loose-leaf TEA in the cup and pouring water on it. While sipping the tea, either discuss your question (if you are reading for someone else) or contemplate your question (if you are reading for yourself). Once the tea is nearly gone, take the cup in your left hand and slowly turn it around three times counterclockwise. Then place a napkin on the top of the cup and turn the cup upside down on the napkin. Keep the handle facing you, turn the cup over, and begin reading the shapes inside the cup.

There are beautiful cups made specifically for reading tea leaves, which have designs inside to assist with interpretations. For example, there are cups that have the zodiac wheel in them to assist with timing and connect astrology to shapes in the cup. There are also cups with numbers, symbols, and even images of cards in them, all meant to support in interpreting the tea leaves in an enriching and in-depth manner.

Interpretations for shapes in the teacup can be found in a variety of tasseography books and through a quick online search; however, you may find that certain shapes symbolize something special to you that go beyond the traditional interpretations. Reading tea leaves can almost feel like an inkblot test—you may see one shape in the leaves, while someone sees something different. It takes time to feel comfortable reading tea leaves, so take time to reflect on it and write about what you see, thinking about what the leaves could mean to you before turning to a list of ready-made messages.

Sandra Mariah Wright and Leanne Marrama make an excellent observation about how it initially feels to look at tea leaves in the bottom of a teacup for the first time in their book, *Reading the Leaves*: "Most of the forms you will recognize can be broken up into categories like nature, animals, objects, body parts, and numbers and letters. Through meditation, practice, and getting clear on your intention, the images will begin to appear more easily and their messages will make themselves known. The leaves will begin to speak to you" (38).

INTERPRETATION

Here are some simple interpretations to keep in mind:

◊ One way to look at timing is to see the handle of the teacup as the present, the left side the past, and the right side the future.

◊ Alternately, consider the following timing technique described by Gregory Lee White and Catherine Yronwode in *The Stranger in the Cup*. According to them, tasseographer Ron Martin Shank, would read timing in the tea leaf reading by holding the teacup handle at the "twelve o'clock position and, proceeding clockwise, silently count off the twelve spaces as months of the year"(41).

SIGNS & MEANINGS

Look for letters and numbers in the patterns and determine if they have any significance to the reading. Look for common shapes like squares, circles, arrows, triangles, and stars. If you are familiar with astrological symbols, you may want to search for them in your tea. Their characteristics may play a role in the reading; the same can be said for tarot symbols—if you are familiar with cups, pentacles, wands, and swords, they can be used to help deepen the meanings of readings as well.

† ARROWS indicate news, usually not good news. An arrow pointing toward the handle indicates bad news to the person getting the reading. An arrow pointing away from the handle means the person is going to be giving bad news.

† CHAINS represent responsibilities or karma.

† CIRCLES indicate success. A circle with a dot in it could indicate a baby.

† CROSSES indicate trouble and worry.

† **Hearts** indicate love.

† **Letters** (as in the written letter) indicate news.

† **Lines** indicate a journey. Straight lines are peaceful journeys, while wavy lines are difficult journeys.

† **Question Marks** warn to be careful.

† **Spirals** indicate a creative period.

† **Squares** indicate protection and security, and in some cases, show restriction.

† **Stars** indicate good luck.

† **Triangles** indicate good luck.

† **Wheels** indicate motion forward.

† A **single leaf** floating on the tea indicates money coming in.

† Look for **Animals**, **People**, or **Nature** (mountains, waves, trees, etc.):

‡ A **Bee** can indicate gossip.

‡ A **Cat** seated is a sign of good luck.

‡ A **Dog** indicates a good, loyal friend.

‡ A **Duck** indicates money on the way.

‡ A **Fish** indicates blessings.

‡ A **Horse** indicates news on the way.

‡ A **Pig** indicates greediness.

DIVINATION
WITH COFFEE GROUNDS

Much like tea leaves, **coffee grounds** can be read as well. The divination of reading coffee grounds dates to the Ottoman Empire in Turkey. Use finely ground Turkish or Greek coffee for a coffee reading. Coffee is traditionally brewed in a copper pot called a cezve. Brew two teaspoons coffee and stir until there is a foam at the top. Pour into small light-colored cups, like a demitasse cup that come with a saucer.

Drink the coffee until there is very little left, about a fifth of the coffee remaining. Hold the cup while thinking of a question, then place the saucer on the top of the cup. Swirl the cup three times counterclockwise, then, with the saucer still covering the top of the cup, turn the cup upside down onto it. Return the cup upright and read the grounds in a similar fashion to reading tea leaves.

SIGNS & MEANINGS

Here are some things to look for when reading coffee grounds:

◊ If there are large chunks of coffee grounds remaining on the saucer, you will find relief from troubles.

◊ If coffee drips onto the saucer when you lift the cup, there is sadness ahead.

† A RING symbolizes marriage.

† A BROKEN RING symbolizes a breakup.

† A BIRD brings a message of good news.

† A FISH brings a message pertaining to career.

† A FLOWER brings messages of happiness.

† A HEART brings messages of love.

† A MOUNTAIN indicates obstacles ahead.

† A SQUARE represents a new home or residence.

MY HOPE IS THAT YOU ARE ENCOURAGED AND excited to try out new and unique forms of divination after reading this book. All divination holds its own unique value and the form that is best for you is the one that you are most drawn to. To be part of this human experience is to always be in wonder of what we cannot see, to be fascinated by those secrets that awaken our imagination and inspire us to further explore the realms of the unknown. Divination helps us explore those unchartered territories; it offers insight and wisdom where it is needed and awakens curiosity about things that may not be available for us to view in plain sight. To practice divination is to be inspired; it is a means to converse with divinity and the universe. Divination has the power to offer hope and provide suggestions which can bring about new perspectives and solutions. As a diviner, you communicate to deity through the rituals of divination, looking beyond the obvious and allowing the mysterious world of symbols and omens to awaken magical potential from deep within.

ACKNOWLEDGEMENTS

FIRST, AND FOREMOST, I WOULD LIKE TO THANK Tonya Brown for all of her support over the years. She is brilliant, patient, one of my favorite people, and one of my closest friends. I am so grateful for her editorial eyes on this book and her all of her encouragement in my writing endeavors. I would also like to thank the *Witch Way Magazine* and *Witch Daily Show* communities, who are supportive, kind, and knowledgeable. Another gracious thank you to Paul Flagg for editing this book, as well also for offering me a platform to teach tarot at the Boston Public Library. Thank you to Michael Herkes for being such a supportive and kind friend – his ambition and energy has been an inspiration all along. Thank you to Mandy and Natty at Extraordinary Oracle for always reminding me to hustle harder. As always, thank you to my family: they have been there to support me and celebrate the milestones I've reached. I want to especially thank my mother and my Aunt Susan for sharing stories with my about their grandfather seeing auras. Thank you to my "girls" on the Islands: Joy, Kelly, and Jen. And, thank you to Ben for constantly supporting me, believing in me, and helping to create a spiritual and magical world.

APPENDIX 1: GLOSSARY

AEROMANCY: Divination with clouds, thunder, lightning, and phenomena that occur in the sky.

ALEUROMANCY: Divination with flour.

ASTRAGALOMANCY: Divination with dice, originally done with a set of marked knucklebones.

ASTROLOGY: The observation of celestial bodies; their motions and placements throughout the sky in complex charting to interpret an individual's personality traits, determine energetic influences during a certain time period, and create predictions about events for a person and/or the world in general.

AUSTROMANCY: Divination with wind.

AUTOMATIC WRITING: A method of using writing as a way to channel spiritual messages.

BIBLIOMANCY: Divination of opening a book to a random place and reading that passage as a fortune.

CAPNOMANCY: Divination with fire smoke.

CARTOMANCY: Divination using cards, such as tarot, oracle, Lenormand, or playing cards.

CERAUNOMANCY: Divination with thunder and lightning.

CEROMANCY: Divination with wax shapes.

CHEIROMANCY: Divination of the lines and markings on a hand – also known as palmistry.

CLEROMANCY: Divination by casting of lots. This term encompasses the casting of dice, stones, shells, beans, coins, dominoes, and so on.

CROMNIOMANCY: Divination with onions.

DAPHNOMANCY: Divination of throwing bay laurel leaves onto a fire.

DOWSING: Divination seeking water, oil, grave sites, vibrations, or random objects.

FLOROMANCY: Divination using flowers.

GRAPHOLOGY: The analysis and study of handwriting to determine a writer's personality, mood, feelings, or life skills.

HALOMANCY: Divination with salt.

HYDROMANCY: Divination with water.

LECANOMANCY: Divination with oil on water.

LIBANOMANCY: Divination with smoke from incense.

LITHOMANCY: Divination by casting precious stones, crystals, or gems.

MEDIUMSHIP: A psychic experience of connecting with and communicating with the spirits of the dead.

NEPHELOMANCY: Divination with clouds.

NUMEROLOGY: The analysis and study of numbers, assigning numbers to spiritual lessons, personality traits, and mystical messages.

ONEIROMANCY: Divination of dreams.

OOMANCY: Divining with an egg white.

OOMANTIA: Divining with an eggshell.

OOSCOPY: Divination with an entire egg.

ORNITHOMANCY: Divination with birds, also known as augury.

PESSOMANCY: Divination of pebbles or beans, sometimes known as psephomancy.

PLASTROMANCY: Divination of turtle shells, as done by the ancient Chinese.

PSYCHOMETRY: A practice of holding or touching an object in an attempt to receive psychic messages from it.

PYROMANCY: Divination with fire.

QUERCUSMANCY: Divination using acorns or oak trees.

SCRYING: Divination by gazing into reflective surfaces to receive psychic impressions.

SELENOMANCY: Divination with the moon.

SPODOMANCY: Divination with ashes.

TASSEOGRAPHY: Divination by reading tea leaves.

TIROMANCY: Divination with cheese.

BEGINNER DECK
RECOMMENDATIONS

Basic tarot decks tend to be inspired by the Rider-Waite deck. Some decks will so closely mimic the Rider-Waite deck that they are known as "Rider-Waite clones." I use a version of a Rider-Waite deck called the "Smith Waite Centennial," which honors Pamela Colman Smith, the illustrator of the original deck. I recommend starting with a deck that is inspired by the Rider-Waite deck, simply because many guidebooks draw their interpretive inspiration from it. This is simply a recommendation, however. As always, you should pick a deck you are deeply drawn to.

◊ Aquarian Tarot

◊ Connolly Tarot

◊ Dreaming Way Tarot

◊ Epicurean Tarot

◊ Fenestra Tarot

◊ Golden Tarot

◊ Hanson-Roberts Tarot

◊ Herbal Tarot

◊ Modern Witch Tarot

◊ Morgan-Greer Tarot

◊ Mythic Tarot

◊ Radiant Rider Waite

◊ Revelations Tarot

◊ Rider-Waite Tarot

◊ Robin-Wood Tarot

◊ Sacred Isle Tarot

◊ Smith Waite Centennial Tarot

◊ Sun and Moon Tarot

◊ Tarot of a Moon Garden

◊ Tarot of the Cat People

◊ Tarot of the New Vision

◊ Thelema Tarot

◊ Universal Tarot

◊ Witches Tarot

INTERMEDIATE
AND ADVANCED DECKS

Although I say you should always work with a deck you are drawn to, I consider these decks better for intermediate and advanced readers, as they stray away from the imagery often depicted in Rider-Waite and decks inspired by it. You may find these decks have developed interpretations, symbols, and themes that are more challenging to use until you have a stronger grasp of tarot.

◊ After Tarot
◊ Alice Tarot
◊ Art of Life Tarot
◊ Bohemian Tarot
◊ Celestial Tarot
◊ Chrysalis Tarot
◊ Commonwealth Tarot
◊ Cosmic Tarot
◊ Deviant Moon Tarot
◊ Druidcraft Tarot
◊ Enchanted Tarot
◊ Ethereal Visions
◊ Fountain Tarot
◊ Ghosts and Spirits Tarot
◊ Gilded Tarot
◊ Goddess Tarot
◊ Haindl Tarot
◊ Halloween Tarot
◊ Illest Tarot
◊ Illuminati Tarot
◊ Legacy of the Divine Tarot

◊ Legend: Arthurian Tarot
◊ Linestrider Tarot
◊ Luminous Spirit Tarot
◊ Mary-El Tarot
◊ Muse Tarot
◊ Night Sun Tarot
◊ Ostara Tarot
◊ Pagan Otherworlds Tarot
◊ Prisma Visions Tarot
◊ Sacred Circle Tarot
◊ Starchild Tarot
◊ Tarot Illuminati
◊ Tarot of Delphi
◊ Tarot of the Hidden Realm
◊ Tarot of the Sevenfold Mystery
◊ True Heart Intuitive Tarot
◊ Voyager Tarot
◊ White Magic Tarot Spells
◊ Wildwood Tarot
◊ Wild Unknown Tarot
◊ Wooden Tarot

There are so many incredible and fascinating oracle decks out there that it is important for me to preface this list with saying: please keep your eyes out for new creations online. Kickstarter usually has new campaigns for funding both tarot and oracle decks. What I am sharing with you are decks I have been recommended by other oracle readers in my pursuit to collect all of the pretty things.

◊ Angels and Ancestors
◊ Animal Spirit
◊ Beyond Lemuria
◊ Compendium of Constellations
◊ Divine Connection
◊ Earthbound Oracle
◊ Earthly Souls and Spirits
◊ Enchanted Blossoms
◊ Extraordinary Oracle
◊ Faceted Garden
◊ Flower Medicine
◊ Goddess Power Oracle
◊ Hedgewitch Botanical
◊ Illuminated Earth Oracle
◊ Jade Oracle
◊ Literary Witches Oracle
◊ Magick of You Oracle
◊ Materia Medica Oracle

◊ Moonology Oracle
◊ Neon Visions Oracle
◊ Nocturna Oracle
◊ Rebel Deck
◊ Sacred Destiny
◊ Sacred Self Care Oracle
◊ Spirit Cats
◊ Starseed Oracle
◊ Supra Oracle
◊ Tamed Wild Rituals
◊ The Crystal Grid Oracle
◊ The Druid Plant Oracle
◊ Threads of Fate Oracle
◊ Wild Unknown Archetypes
◊ Witch Daily Oracle
◊ Working Your Light
◊ Yogic Path

These are a few spreads that you can use with your tarot or oracle cards, or perhaps any lots like ogham or runes that you are casting if you wish.

DAILY LESSON SPREAD

This is an excellent spread to work with daily to get divination practice. It will allow you to prepare for the day and feel ready to live it to the fullest. Do this at the beginning of the day, and make sure to take notes. At the end of the day, review your reading to see how it may have mirrored your day.

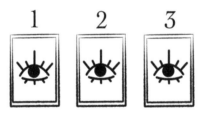

(1) VALUABLE LESSON FOR THE DAY: This card/lot represents a lesson you will be able to learn today. This is something that helps you feel more aware, connected, and knowledgeable.

(2) IMPORTANT EVENT FOR THE DAY: This card/lot represents something special that is going to happen.

(3) SPECIAL MESSAGE: This card/lot represents a special message from a spirit guide or ancestor that you work with. Use these as encouraging words or work with the symbolism and stories for what was drawn in this position.

PERSONAL CHECK-IN SPREAD

This spread originally appeared in *Witch Way Magazine* and is used as a way to check in with yourself and engage with how you are feeling, hopefully guiding you into feeling centered and present with yourself and focused on your wellbeing.

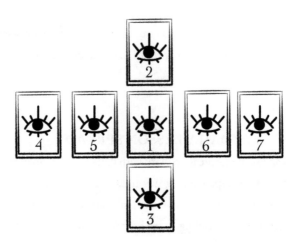

(1) PRESENT MOMENT: This card/lot shows what is surrounding you currently and influencing your wellbeing.

(2) MENTAL CHECK-IN: This card/lot shows what you are thinking about and how to calm your mind.

(3) EMOTIONAL CHECK-IN: This card/lot shows you are feeling emotionally and how to soothe difficult feelings.

(4) LOVING CHECK-IN: This card/lot shows you how love is appearing in your life and how you can bring more love in.

(5) FINANCIAL CHECK-IN: This card/lot shows how finances are going in your life and what you can do to gain more abundance.

(6) SPIRITUAL CHECK-IN: This card/lot shows you how you are feeling spiritually and how you can enhance spirit in your life.

(7) FUTURE EVENTS: This card/lot shows a special event, person, date, or energy that will appear in your life in the near future.

FULL MOON SPIRITUAL SOUL SPREAD

This is an excellent spread for any reader of this book, as it allows you to examine your magical gifts, your psychic abilities, and your spiritual development. I call this the "Full Moon Spread" because it aligns with the powers of the moon and is a useful spread to cast each full moon.

(1) **YOUR UNIQUE MAGICAL GIFTS**: This card/lot examines how you are a magical creature and the magical gifts you are enjoying in this lifetime.

(2) **BENEFICIAL SPIRITUAL PRACTICE**: This card/lot examines spiritual practices, rituals, or activities that will help to soothe your soul and lead you onto a path of peaceful enlightenment.

(3) **POWERFUL SPIRITUAL STUDIES**: This card/lot examines things that you can study to support your spiritual development. You may wish to study the lessons and symbols in this card/lot or look to its interpretation to allow you to find the guidance you need.

(3) **PSYCHIC DEVELOPMENT**: This card/lot examines what you can do to develop your psychic abilities. Use this card as a support in helping you see where your psychic gifts are, how they help you, and how you can use them to their fullest extent.

(5) **LUNAR SOUL**: This card/lot is a message from divinity, specifically a divine or ancestral spirit that aligns with the workings of the moon. This card/lot should offer ways to find comfort and magic through the following moon cycle.

SIMPLE PAST-PRESENT-FUTURE SPREAD

In this spread, you will simply deal three cards or lots to read:

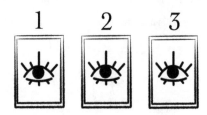

(1) THE PAST

(2) THE PRESENT

(3) THE FUTURE

For more spreads, visit my Instagram page at @kikiscauldron.

I have been so blessed to be able to work alongside some of the most brilliant, gifted, and talented people. My hope here is to share with you some of the things that bring magic into my life and may inspire your divination practices.

WITCH WAY MAGAZINE: *Witch Way Magazine* is a beautiful magical community for people from all magical and metaphysical paths in the world. If you are looking for a welcoming community of witches, connect with *Witch Way Magazine*, where the gates are wide open.

LIMINAL EARTH: Liminal Earth is a fascinating and interactive online map that catalogs weird events, high strangeness, and supernatural encounters around the world. If you've had a vivid dream or a particularly impressive divination session, share your story on their map.

RADIANT COACHES ACADEMY: Radiant Coaches Academy is an accredited holistic life-coaching training. If you would like to give a proactive and supportive slant to your divination readings, consider looking into life coaching to deepen your supportive coaching and active-listening skills.

PAGAN UNITY FESTIVAL: Tish Owen of Goddess and the Moon has invited me year after year to participate in this powerful Pagan festival, which happens annually in the woods of Tennessee. This is a wonderful space for people to gather, study, and celebrate witchcraft, magic, and divination.

Flatwoods Fawn: Flatwoods Fawn is my favorite jewelry line, creating bold pieces with crystals perfect for the bohemian spirit. There are also special pieces that celebrate the zodiac signs.

Folklore Thursday: Folklore Thursday is a weekly event on Twitter hosted by Folklorists Dee Dee Chainey and Willow Winsham. Every week you will hear about folklore from around the world, from a diverse range of cultures. Oftentimes, people will chime in with superstitions and folkloric divination.

Insight Timer: Insight Timer is an active meditation app that you can keep on your phone. There are thousands of recordings of soothing music and guided meditations to walk you through a present and profound experience. My favorite teachers, who have metaphysically minded meditations are Rachel Hillary and Sarah Robinson.

My Friends with Podcasts: I am so grateful to have many friends hosting genius podcasts. The ones that fit into the magical and paranormal realms that I recommend listening to include *My Haunted Life, Some Other Sphere, Paranormal Patio, The Witch Daily Show, Two Witches Podcast, Paranormal Patio, Conspirinormal Podcast, Binnall of America, Penny Royal, and The Eternal Void, But With Jazz.*

The Traveling Museum of the Paranormal and Occult: This incredible Patreon is run by Greg and Dana Newkirk, who are best known for their paranormal series *Hellier*. The series itself introduces viewers to the ideas of synchronicities. Dana utilizes tarot in her paranormal investigations, and the couple are open to using psychic techniques as methods for receiving information on their cases. Their Patreon allows you to follow their work, which includes watching live investigations, in which viewers often share their own psychic impressions and messages they've received from divination work.

The Hermit Priestess: My friend M. Kyndyll Lackey is a phenomenal writer and tarot reader. She works with the Thoth deck and utilizes claircognizant abilities to support her readings. Her writing combines her knowledge of tarot and astrology to give insightful wisdom.

Melanie Bresnan: Melanie brings her spiritual reflections into her magical music and illustrations. Most recently, she created a beautiful collection of songs and corresponding artwork inspired by the tarot.

AromaG's Botanica: AromaG's Botanica is a go-to metaphysical shop located in Nashville, TN. Greg and Roy Hamilton-White run the shop and share their incredible handmade products, ranging from delicious-smelling oils to spiritually-inspired soaps. They also blend a tea made specifically for tasseography. AromaG's supports so many talented locals and has created a supportive community of magically-minded people.

Johnny Dombrowski: Johnny created the original cover for *A Curious Future*. He is a talented and successful illustrator, having had his work featured in *Entertainment Weekly, Village Voice, DC Comics, the Boston Globe*, and more. He also happens to be my brother!

Josh Stewart: Josh Stewart is a photographer based on Tybee Island. While he may be best known for his stunning sunset and nighttime photography, he also took my portrait for this book.

A Special Thank You to the "Divination Experts" I spoke to for this book:
Tonya A. Brown: witchwaymagazine.com
Michael Herkes: theglamwitch.com
Suzie Kerr Wright: astrogirl12.com
Ms. Kathryn: neworleanshairwitch.com

ASTROLOGY

Bloch, Douglas and Demetra George: *Astrology for Yourself: A Workbook for Personal Transformation.* Ibis Press: Lake Worth, Florida, 2006.

Cunningham, Donna. *Moon Signs: The Key to Your Inner Life.* Ballantine Books, 1988.

Guttman, Ariel and Kenneth Johnson. Mythic Astrology: Internalizing the Planetary Powers. Llewellyn Publications: St. Paul, MN, 2004.

Hering, Amy. *Astrology of the Moon: An Illuminating Journey Through the Signs & Houses.* Llewellyn Publications, 2010.

Eddington, Louise. *The Complete Guide to Astrology: Understanding Yourself, Your Signs, and Your Birth Chart.* Rockridge Press: Emeryville, CA, 2020.

Hand, Robert. *Planets in Transit: Life Cycles for Living.* Whitford Press: Atglen, Pennsylvania, 1976.

Hickey, Isabel. M. *Astrology: A Cosmic Science.* CRCS Publications, 2011.

Leek, Sybil. *Moon Signs: Lunar Astrology.* Berkley Publishing Corporation, 1977.

Lewi, Grant. *Astrology for the Millions.* Llewellyn Publications, 1990.

March, Marion and Joan McEvers. *The Only Way to Learn Astrology, Vol. 1: Basic Principles.* Starcrafts Publications, 2008.

Nicholas, Chani. *You Were Born For This: Astrology for Radical Self Acceptance.* Harper One, 2020.

AURAS

Bruyere, Rosalyn. *Wheels of Light: Chakras, Auras, and the Healing Energy of the Body.* Fireside, 1994.

McLaren, Karla. *Your Aura and Your Chakras.* Samuel Weiser Inc., 1998.

AUTOMATIC WRITING

Richardson, Irene. *Learn How to Do Automatic Writing: A Step by Step Course to Help You Access Higher Realms of the Mind, Body and Spirit.* Crystal Forests, 2008.

BONE CASTING

Jackson, Michele. *Bones, Shells, and Curios: A Contemporary Method of Casting the Bones.* Lucky Mojo Curio Company, 2014.

Yronwode, Catherine. *Throwing the Bones: How to Foretell the Future with Bones, Shells, and Nuts.* Lucky Mojo Curio Company, 2012.

CRYSTALS
AND LITHOMANCY

Cunningham, Scott. *Cunningham's Encyclopedia of Crystal, Gem and Metal Magic.* Llewellyn, 2002.

Dunwich, Gerina. *Dunwich's Guide to Gemstone Sorcery: Using Stones for Spells, Amulets, Rituals, and Divination.* New Page Books, 2003.

Eason, Cassandra. *Cassandra Eason's Healing Crystals.* Collins & Brown, New York, 2015.

Simmons, Robert & Naisha Ahsian. *The Book of Stones,* 2nd ed. Heaven and Earth Publishing: East Montpelier, VT, 2015.

Wimmer, Gary L. *Lithomancy: The Psychic Art of Reading Stones.* Gary L. Wimmer, 2010.

DOWSING

Eason, Cassandra. *The Art of the Pendulum: Simple techniques to help you make decisions, find lost objects, and channel healing energies*. Weiser Books, 1999.

Graves, Tom. The Diviner's Handbook: A Guide to the Timeless Art of Dowsing. Destiny Books, 1986.

Hunt, Brenda. *A Beginner's Guide to Pendulum Dowsing*. CreateSpace Independent Publishing, 2012.

Webster, Richard. *Dowsing for Beginners: How to Find Water, Wealth & Lost Objects*. Llewellyn Publications, 2012.

DREAMS

DeBord, J.M. *The Dream Interpretation Dictionary: Symbols, Signs, and Meanings*. Visible Ink Press, 2017.

Johnson, Robert A. *Inner Work: Using Dreams and Active Imagination for Personal Growth*. Harper & Row, 1989.

Milligan, Ira. *The Ultimate Guide to Understanding the Dreams you Dream*. Destiny Image   Publishers, 2012.

Shafer, Scott M. *Awakening Dreams and Night Visions, Towards a New Paradigm*. Bookstand Publishing, 2007.

GENERAL GUIDEBOOKS

Bluestone, Sarvananda. *How to Read Signs and Omens in Everyday Life*. Destiny Books, 2002.

Brown, Colette. *How to Read an Egg: Divination for the Easily Bored*. Dodona Books, 2014.

Buckland, Raymond. *Secrets of Gypsy Fortune Telling*. Llewellyn Publications, 1988.

Buckland, Raymond. *The Fortune-Telling Book: The Encyclopedia of Divination and Soothsaying*. Visible Ink Press, 2004.

Cunningham, Scott. *The Art of Divination*. The Crossing Press, 1993.

Daniels, Cora Linn and C.M. Stevens, editors. *Encyclopedia of Superstitions, Folklore, and the Occult Sciences of the World, Vol. 2.* University Press of the Pacific, 2003.

Dean, Liz. *The Ultimate Guide to Divination: The Beginner's Guide to Using Cards, Crystals, Runes, Palmistry, and more for Insight and Predicting the Future.* Quatro Publishing, 2018.

Dunwich, Gerina. *A Wiccan's Guide to Prophecy and Divination.* Citadel Press, 1997.

Fenton, Sasha. *Fortune Teller's Handbook: 20 Fun and Easy Techniques for Predicting the Future.* Hampton Roads Publishing, 2017.

Pennick, Nigel. *Magical Alphabets.* Weiser Books, 1992.

Pickover, Clifford A. *Dreaming of the Future: The Fantastic Story of Prediction.* Prometheus Books, 2001.

Webster, Richard. *Llewellyn's Complete Book of Divination.* Llewellyn, 2017.

GRAPHOLOGY AND HANDWRITING ANALYSIS

Amend, Karen Kristin, and Mary S. Ruiz. *Handwriting Analysis: The Complete Basic Book.* Newcastle Publishing, 1986.

LENORMAND

Katz, Marcus and Tali Goodwin. *Learning Lenormand: Traditional Fortune Telling for Modern Life.* Llewellyn Publications: Woodbury, MN 2013.

Matthews, Caitlin. *The Complete Lenormand Oracle Handbook: Reading the Language and Symbols of the Cards.* Destiny Books: Rochester, VT.

MEDIUMSHIP

Brennan, J.H. *Whisperers: The Secret History of the Spirit World.* The Overlook Press, 2013.

Buckland, Raymond. *Buckland's Book of Spirit Communications.* Llewellyn, 2004.

Buckland, Raymond. *The Spirit Book: The Encyclopedia of Clairvoyance, Channeling, and Spirit Communication.* Visible Ink Press, 2005.

Dillard, Sherrie. *You Are a Medium: Discover Your Natural Abilities to Communicate with the Other Side.* Llewellyn Publications, 2013.

Dione, Danielle. Magickal Mediumship. Llewellyn Publications, 2020.

Palm, Diana. *Mediumship Scrying & Transfiguration for Beginners: A Guide to Spirit Communication.* Llewellyn Publications, 2017.

Tyson, Jenny. *Spiritual Alchemy: Scrying, Spirit Communication, and Alchemical Wisdom.* Llewellyn Publications, 2016.

NUMEROLOGY

Goodwin, Matthew Oliver. *Numerology, The Complete Guide: Volume 1.* New Page Books, 2005.

Javane. Faith and Dusty Bunker. *Numerology and the Divine Triangle.* Whitford Press, 1979.

Keller, Joyce and Jack. *The Complete Book of Numerology.* Macmillan Publishers, 2015.

Woodward, Joy. *A Beginner's Guide to Numerology: Decode Relationships, Maximize Opportunities, and Discover Your Destiny.* Rockridge Press: Emeryville, CA, 2019.

OGHAM, DRUIDIC AND CELTIC STUDIES

Blamires, Steve. *Celtic Tree Mysteries: Practical Druid Magic and Divination.* Llewellyn Publications, 1997.

Carr-Gomm, Philip. *The Druid Tradition.* Element Books Limited, 1991.

Forest, Danu. *Celtic Tree Magic: Ogham Lore and Druid Mysteries.* Llewellyn Publications, 2014.

Hutton, Ronald. *Blood & Mistletoe: The History of the Druids in Britain.* Yale University Press, 2009.

Kynes, Sandra. *Whispers from the Woods: The Lore and Magic of Trees.*

Llewellyn Publications, 2006.

Laure, Erynn Rowan. *Ogam: Weaving Word Wisdom*. Megalithica Books, 2007.

Mountfort, Paul Rhys. *Ogam: The Celtic Oracle of Trees: Understanding, Casting, and Interpreting the Ancient Druidic Alphabet.* Destiny Books, 2002.

Weber, Courtney. *Brigid: History, Mystery, and Magick of the Celtic Goddess.* Weiser Books, 2015.

PALMISTRY

Altman, Nathaniel. *Palmistry: The Universal Guide.* Guapo Publishing, 2017.

Benham, William G. *The Benham Book of Palmistry.* New Page Books, 2006.

Campbell, Edward D. *The Encyclopedia of Palmistry.* Perigree Trade, 1996.

Goldberg, Ellen. *The Art and Science of Hand Reading: Classical Methods for Self-Discovery through Palmistry.* Destiny Books, 2016.

Levine, Roz. *Palmistry: How to Chart the Lines of Your Life.* Touchstone Books, 1993.

PSYCHIC DEVELOPMENT

Auryn, Mat. Psychic Witch: A Metaphysical Guide to Meditation, Magick & Manifestation. Llewellyn, 2020.

Eason, Cassandra. *A Complete Guide to Psychic Development.* Piatkus Books, 2002.

Friedlander, John and Gloria Hemsher. *Basic Psychic Development.* Weiser Books, 2012.

Katz, Debra Lynne. *You Are Psychic: The Art of Clairvoyant Reading and Healing.* Llewellyn, 2004.

Wolf, Stacey. *Get Psychic! Discover Your Hidden Powers.* Warner Books, 2001.

RUNES

MacLeod, Mindy and Bernard Mees. *Runic Amulets and Magic Objects.* Boydell Press, 2006.

Mountfort, Paul Rhys. *Nordic Runes: Understanding, Casting and, Interpreting the Ancient Viking Oracle.* Inner Traditions/Bear & Company, 2003.

Page, R.I. *Runes.* University of California Press, 1987.

Paxson, Diana. *Taking Up the Runes: A Complete Guide to Using Runes in Spells, Ritual, Divination, and Magic.* Weiser Books, 2005.

Plowright, Swevn. *The Rune Primer: A Down to Earth Guide to the Runes.* Sweyn Plowright, 2006.

Spurkland, Terje. *Norwegian Runes and Runic Inscriptions.* Translated by Betsy van der Hoek, The Boydell Press, 2005.

SCRYING

Andrews, Ted. *Crystal Balls and Crystal Bowls: Tools for Ancient Scrying and Modern Seership.* Llewellyn Publications, 2004.

Eason, Cassandra. *Scrying the Secrets of the Future.* New Page Books, 2007.

Guiley, Rosemary Ellen. *The Art of Black Mirror Scrying. Visionary Living Inc.,* 2016.

TAROT

Bunning, Joan. *Learning the Tarot: Tarot Book for Beginners.* Weiser Books, 1998.

Greer, Mary K. *Tarot for Yourself, Second Edition.* New Page Books, 2002.

Huggins, Kim. *Tarot 101: Mastering the Art of Reading the Cards.* Llewellyn Publications, 2010.

Pamita, Madame. *Madame Pamita's Magical Tarot: Using the Cards to Make Your Dreams Come True.* Weiser Books, 2018.

Pollack, Rachel. *Seventy-Eight Degrees of Wisdom: A Book of Tarot.*

Weiser Books, 2007.

Tea, Michelle. *Modern Tarot: Connecting with Your Higher Self through the Wisdom of the Cards.* Harper One, 2017.

Weber, Courtney. *Tarot for One: The Art of Reading for Yourself.* Weiser Books, 2016.

Wen, Benebell. *Holistic Tarot: An Integrative Approach to Using Tarot for Personal Growth.* North Atlantic Books, 2015.

TASSEOGRAPHY

Fenton, Sasha. *Tea Cup Reading: A Quick Guide to Tasseography.* Weiser Books, 2002.

White, Gregory Lee and Catherine Yronwode. *The Stranger in the Cup: How to Read Your Luck and Fate in the Tea Leaves.* Lucky Mojo Curio Company: Forestville, California, 2020.

Wright, Sandra Mariah and Leanne Marrama. *Reading the Leaves: An Intuitive Guide to the Ancient Art of Modern Magic of Tea Leaf Divination.* Tarcher Perigee, 2020.

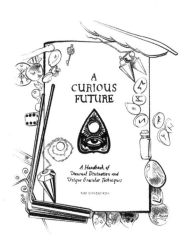

ABOUT THE AUTHOR

KIKI DOMBROWSKI is a spiritual researcher and explorer who has spent her life studying mythology, magic, tarot, witchcraft, and the supernatural. She has a Master's Degree in Medieval English from the University of Nottingham and a Bachelor's Degree in English and Creative Writing from Southern Connecticut State University.

She currently lives in Savannah where she is a professional tarot card reader, certified life coach, and writer. Prior to living in Savannah, Kiki lived in Nashville, where she taught numerous courses on divination and witchcraft at Pagan Unity Festival, Pagan Pride Day, AromaG's, and Mystical Heart Spiritual Center. Kiki has been a contributing writer for *Witch Way Magazine* for over five years. She has also contributed writing to the *Wicca Book of Spells Witches' Planner 2021* and *Witch Way's Book of 100 Love Spells.* Her next book projects include a revision of *Eight Extraordinary Days*, her book on the Witches' Wheel of the Year, and a new book on tarot. She has been a guest on numerous podcasts including *The Witch Daily Show, Some Other Sphere Podcast,* and *The Conspirinormal Podcast.*

For more information visit her website kikidombrowski.com. You can follow her on Twitter @KikiD333, or on Instagram @KikisCauldron.